MY TREASURY
of
CHAPLETS

Patricia S. Quintiliani

Our Lady of Fatima

MY TREASURY
of
CHAPLETS

Eighth, Enlarged Edition

Compiled from Approved Sources
by
Patricia S. Quintiliani

Introduction
by
Father Vincent P. Miceli

THE RAVENGATE PRESS
Still River, Massachusetts

ISBN: 0-911218-46-7
Library of Congress Catalog Card Number: 91-134199

Published and Distributed by
The Ravengate Press
252 Still River Road, P. O. Box 49
Still River, Massachusetts 01467-0049
1-800-344-6736

Also Distributed by
Religious Art, Inc.
276 Greenpoint Avenue
Broooklyn, NY 11222
1-800-991-1211

Photographs by Ernest J. Quintiliani

Illustrations on pages 10, 114, 126, 306 and 316
from *The Rosary*, by permission of The Benedict
Press, 8711 Muensterschwartzach Abbey, Germany.

Cover Photograph:
Our Lady of the Rosary of Pompeii

MANUFACTURED IN CANADA

CONTENTS

INTRODUCTION

A chaplet is a devotion of prayers centered around the recitation of a special type of rosary in honor of some member of the Holy Trinity, of Jesus Christ, of His Holy Mother, of the Angels and of the Saints. The whole purpose of a chaplet is either to initiate a special devotion to the Holy Person to whom the prayers are directed or to revive a devotion to that person. Often these devotions have been neglected because of a loss of faith or because of the discontinuance of a religious tradition due to a secularistic atmosphere.

Then too, devotional chaplets are begun to foster new devotions in the Church, e.g., devotion to the Divine Mercy, to the Sacred Heart, to the Holy Angels, to the Holy Face, to the Holy Spirit, to St. Anthony of Padua, to the Precious Blood, to the Blessed Sacrament, to the Seven Dolors of Mary, to the Infant Jesus, to St. Michael the Archangel. Holy chaplets are prayerful means to meet the trials of the Church in every era of her historical battle against the powers of darkness. Just as Satan seduces mankind to accept new popular habits of heresy and moral corruption such as neo-modernism, contraception, premarital sex, abortion, divorce and remarriage, euthanasia, etc., so God arouses His Church to counter-attack these corruptions with the fire of zeal developed from the devotional chaplets and from the return to the frequent recitation of the Holy Rosary, daily attendance at Holy Mass, frequent confession, Holy Communion and dedication to a way of life totally dedicated to following Christ.

This book, which contains the beautiful prayers of a variety of these holy chaplets, is meant to help the faithful to enter into these prayers and thus grow in union with the Holy Trinity, with Christ, His Holy Mother, the Angels and the Saints. In this way they will grow in holiness themselves and help others on the way to holiness and thereby cooperate with Christ and Mary in the destruction of the Kingdom of Satan.

May this book find a vast and profitable readership.

Father Vincent P. Miceli

PREFACE

All the chaplets in this collection can be recited without the use of chaplet beads. Many require the use of ordinary Rosary beads (the Chaplet of Divine Mercy, the Chaplet to Gain a Great Confidence, the Rosary of the Holy Wounds). Some of the beads are interchangeable. The Little Chaplet of the Holy Ghost can be recited on the Franciscan Crown. Both versions of the Sacred Heart Chaplet can be recited on the same beads. The Rosary of the Tears of Blood can be said on the Rosary of the Seven Sorrows.

A chaplet can be used as a novena on the days preceding the feast of the Saint to whom it is dedicated, or at any time when a favor is needed. The Chaplet of St. Michael is especially recommended daily to pray for the great Archangel's protection for the Church during these trying times. The Little Chaplet of the Holy Ghost is recommended for Sundays or when some important decision must be made. The Blessed Sacrament Beads can be recited on Thursday which is dedicated to the Holy Eucharist. The Chaplet of Little Philomena is recommended before taking an exam; the Chaplet of St. Raphael before traveling.

Mother Catherine Aurelia describes the Precious Blood Chaplet as "an offering of sweet incense to the Sacred Heart of Jesus." If you recite the St. Theresa Chaplet from the ninth to the seventeenth of each month, you should add to your own intentions those of all who are at that time making the novena, thus forming one great prayer in common.

The Catholic Encyclopedia defines a chaplet as a "crown of religious profession." The chaplets are crowns which we can use to bring greater honor and glory to Our Lord, His Blessed Mother, the Angels and the Saints. They also are forming crowns for our own Heavenly Glory, by storing our treasures in heaven.

Last but most important, the Rosary of the Most Blessed Virgin should be recited and meditated on at least once a day!

If we do as Our Lady has advised us (pray, do penance and offer up our daily crosses), can we not help but believe that we will see the Triumph of Her Immaculate Heart in our lifetime?

PREFACE TO THE EIGHTH EDITION

Many changes have taken place in the past nineteen years since I first completed *My Treasury of Chaplets.* So many wonderful graces have come to me through this book that I felt it was time to thank all of you who have read it. I never intended to have this book go any further than family, friends and members of my Apostolate, but God had other plans. He knew what trials and tribulations lay in store for my family, and He planned ahead for us. He has saved us many times over through this book. It has kept a roof over our heads and food on our table. Much more important are the friends we have made and the spiritual blessings we have received. God is truly our "Good God."

Even though Father Vincent Miceli went to his eternal reward several years ago, I have retained the Introduction he wrote for the first edition of this book. Though it was a minor part of his profound spiritual and theological writings, we were truly grateful to him. Father was a close friend, a spiritual mentor and an exemplary priest, and he is missed by all who knew him.

I would like to thank all those who have sent me suggestions, corrections and chaplets that I did not have in earlier editions. I appreciate your interest and the time you took to write me. I have tried my best to make this eighth edition as clear and complete as possible, and I pray that it will be useful to you in your prayer life, your rosary making and the spreading of devotion to Our Lord and Our Lady. May the Triumph of the Immaculate Heart of Mary come soon!

God bless you all!

Patricia S. Quintiliani

The Great Promise

DEDICATION FOR
THE DAYS OF THE WEEK

Sunday . . . . The Holy Trinity

Monday . . . . The Holy Spirit

Tuesday . . . . The Holy Angels

Wednesday . . . . Saint Joseph

Thursday . . . . The Holy Eucharist

Friday . . . . The Sacred Passion

Saturday . . . . The Blessed Virgin

DEDICATIONS FOR
THE MONTHS OF THE YEAR

Since the 16th century Catholic piety has assigned entire months to special devotions. Those given below are the more common ones, and the Holy See has enriched most of these observations with indulgences. In the following list the starred months are those so distinguished.

*January .... The Holy Name of Jesus
February .... The Holy Family
*March .... Saint Joseph
April .... The Blessed Sacrament
*May .... The Blessed Virgin Mary
*June .... The Sacred Heart
*July .... The Precious Blood
*August ... The Immaculate Heart of Mary
*September .... Our Lady of Sorrows or
                 The Holy Guardian Angels†
*October .... The Holy Rosary
*November ...The Holy Souls in Purgatory
*December ... The Immaculate Conception

† According to the custom in certain European countries.

ACT OF CONSECRATION TO THE
MOST SACRED HEART OF JESUS

O most loving Jesus, Redeemer of the human race, behold us humbly prostrate before Your altar. We are Yours and Yours we wish to be. But to be more surely united in You, behold each one of us freely consecrates himself today to Your most Sacred Heart. Many, indeed, have never known You; many, too, despising Your precepts, have rejected You. Have mercy on them all, most merciful Jesus, and draw them to Your Sacred Heart.

Be King, O Lord, not only of the faithful who have never forsaken You, but also of the prodigal children who have abandoned You. Grant that they may quickly return to their Father's house, lest they die of wretchedness and hunger.

Grant, O Lord, to Your Church assurance of freedom and immunity from harm. Give peace and order to all nations. Make the earth resound from pole to pole with one cry: Praise to the Divine Heart that wrought our salvation. To it be glory and honor forever. Amen.

ACT OF CONSECRATION TO THE
IMMACULATE HEART OF MARY

Immaculate Heart of Mary, Queen of heaven and earth, and tender Mother of men, in accordance with your ardent wish made known at Fatima, we consecrate ourselves to you.

Reign over us, dear Mother, that we may be yours in prosperity and in adversity, in joy and in sorrow, in health and in sickness, in life and in death.

Most compassionate Heart of Mary, Queen of Virgins, watch over our minds and hearts and preserve them from the deluge of impurity which you lamented so sorrowfully at Fatima. We want to atone for the many crimes committed against Jesus and you. We want to call down upon our country and the whole world the peace of God in justice and charity.

Therefore, we now promise to imitate your virtues by the practice of a Christian life without regard to human respect.

We resolve to receive Holy Communion regularly and to offer you five decades of the Rosary each day, together with our sacrifices, in the spirit of reparation and penance. Amen.

THE ANGELUS

(This prayer should be recited morning, noon and evening.)

The angel of the Lord declared unto Mary,
And she conceived of the Holy Spirit.

Hail Mary, full of grace, the Lord is with thee; blessed art thou among women, and blessed is the fruit of thy womb, Jesus. Holy Mary, Mother of God, pray for us sinners, now and at the hour of our death. Amen.

Behold the handmaid of the Lord.
Be it done unto me according to thy word.
    Hail Mary. . . .
And the Word was made flesh.
And dwelt among us.
    Hail Mary. . . .
V.–Pray for us, O Holy Mother of God,
R.–That we may be made worthy of the
    promises of Christ.

Let Us Pray

Pour forth, we beseech Thee, O Lord, Thy grace into our hearts that, as we have known the Incarnation of Christ, Thy Son, by the message of an angel, so by His Passion and Cross we may be brought to the glory of His Resurrection. Through the same Christ our Lord. Amen.

REGINA COELI

(This prayer is recited in place of the Angelus, from Easter until Pentecost.)

Queen of heaven, rejoice! Alleluia.
For He Whom thou didst merit to bear.
  Alleluia.
Hath risen as He said. Alleluia.
Pray for us to God. Alleluia.
V. – Rejoice and be glad, O Virgin Mary.
  Alleluia.
R. – Because the Lord is truly risen.
  Alleluia.

Let us Pray

O God, who by the Resurrection of Thy Son, Our Lord Jesus Christ, didst vouchsafe to fill the world with joy, grant, we beseech Thee, that through His Virgin Mother Mary we may have the joys of everlasting life. Through the same Christ our Lord. Amen.

Glory be to the Father, and to the Son, and to the Holy Spirit, as it was in the beginning, is now, and ever shall be, world without end. Amen.

PRAYER TO HONOR
THE NAME OF MARY

O Mary, each time I say your Name, I want to thank the Holy Trinity for having created you so beautiful and full of grace. I want to honor your Immaculate Conception, your Divine Maternity, and your glorious Assumption.

O Mary, each time I say your Name, I want to unite myself with you in co-offering all the Masses which are being celebrated throughout the world, in order to offer to Jesus through your Immaculate Heart my actions, my prayers, my joys and my troubles each and every moment of my life.

O Mary, each time I say your Name, I want to confide to you those whom I love and those to whom I wish to do good, especially: . . .

I wish to receive from Jesus through you all the graces of which I am in need: spiritual graces and temporal favors, especially. . .

O Mary, each time I say your Name, I want to remind you that I am your child and that you are my Mother. Help me as you helped Jesus. Protect me as you protected Jesus.

When I call you, Mary, remember me!

It would be most efficacious to recite this prayer at the beginning of each day, preferably before our daily Rosary or before any of the chaplets in this book. The name of Mary is mentioned no less than 106 times in the Rosary and at least once in most of the chaplets.

CHAPLETS OF OUR LORD, THE BLESSED SACRAMENT AND THE HOLY SPIRIT

The Holy Trinity

LITTLE CHAPLET IN HONOR OF
THE MOST HOLY TRINITY

Through the Five Sacred Wounds of Our Lord in reparation for the crimes of sinners.

On the Cross say:
  Incline unto mine aid, O God,
  O Lord, make haste to help me.

On the *three small beads and on the large beads* say: Glory be to Thee, O most sweet, most noble, resplendent, peaceful, ineffable Trinity. Amen.

On the *small beads* say: Glory, honor and praise be to the great Eternal God. Amen. *(Ten times.)*

Gloria after each decade.

Conclude with three Glorias and the Divine Praises:

  Blessed be God!
  Blessed be His Holy Name!
  Blessed be Jesus Christ, true God and true
      man!
  Blessed be the Name of Jesus!
  Blessed be His Most Sacred Heart!
  Blessed be His Most Precious Blood!

11

Blessed be Jesus in the Most Holy Sacrament of the altar!

Blessed be the Holy Spirit, the Paraclete!

Blessed be the great Mother of God, Mary most Holy!

Blessed be her holy and Immaculate Conception!

Blessed be her glorious Assumption!

Blessed be the name of Mary, Virgin and Mother!

Blessed be Saint Joseph, her most chaste spouse!

Blessed be God in His Angels and in His Saints!

THE ANGELIC TRISAGION

This hymn of praise to the eternal Trinity is the official prayer of the Order of the Blessed Trinity. For centuries the Trinitarians and those affiliated with them have united themselves to the nine choirs of Angels in praising the Trinity.

This chaplet consists of three sets of nine small beads, each set being separated with a large one.

In the name of the Father, and of the Son, and of the Holy Spirit. Amen.

> *V.* O Lord, Thou wilt open my lips.
> *R.* And my mouth shall declare Thy praise.
> *V.* O God, come to my assistance.
> *R.* O Lord, make haste to help me.
> *V.* Glory be to the Father, and to the Son, and to the Holy Spirit.
> *R.* As it was in the beginning, is now, and ever shall be, world without end. Amen.

> *V.* Holy God, Holy Strong One, Holy Immortal One.
> *R.* Have mercy on us. Our Father, etc.

Then repeat nine times:

V. To Thee be praise, to Thee be glory, to
   Thee be thanksgiving through endless
   ages, O Blessed Trinity.
R. Holy, Holy, Holy Lord God of Hosts:
   the heavens and the earth are full of
   Thy glory.

When completed, recite:

V. Glory be to the Father, and to the Son,
   and to the Holy Spirit.
R. As it was in the beginning, is now,
   and ever shall be, world without end.
   Amen.

*The second and third set will be said in the
same way beginning from Holy God, Holy
Strong One, etc.*

*When the third set is completed, recite the fol-
lowing:*

Ant. With all our heart and voice, we acknowledge, we praise and we bless Thee,
God the Father unbegotten; Thee the only
begotten Son; Thee the Holy Spirit the Paraclete, O holy and undivided Trinity. To Thee
be honor and glory forever.

V. Let us bless the Father, the Son, and the Holy Spirit.

R. Let us praise and exalt Him above all forever.

Let us pray.

Almighty and everlasting God, who hast given unto us, Thy servants, grace by the confession of the true faith to acknowledge the glory of the eternal Trinity, and in the power of Thy divine Majesty to worship the Unity; we beseech Thee, that by our steadfastness in this same faith, we may evermore be defended from all adversities. Through Christ our Lord. Amen.

Invocation

Deliver us, save us, vivify us, O Blessed Trinity.

THE CHAPLET OF
DIVINE MERCY

Using ordinary Rosary beads, begin with:

Our Father . . ., Hail Mary . . ., the Creed.

On the large bead before each decade say:

Eternal Father, I offer You the Body and Blood, Soul and Divinity of Your dearly beloved Son, Our Lord Jesus Christ, in atonement for our sins and those of the whole world.

On the ten small beads of each decade:

For the sake of His sorrowful Passion have mercy on us and on the whole world.

Conclude with:

Holy God, Holy Mighty One, Holy Immortal One, have mercy on us and on the whole world. *(Three times).*

(From Divine Mercy in My Soul, the Diary of Blessed Faustina, Note Book I, p. 197.)

+ Imprimatur: Joseph F. Maguire, Bishop of Springfield, Massachusetts, February 2, 1981.

MERCY AND FORGIVENESS CHAPLET

This chaplet was composed by Chorbishop Joseph Saidi of Worcester, Massachusetts. Father Saidi has been a priest for 64 years and was the pastor of Our Lady of Mercy Maronite Catholic Church from 1947 until his recent retirement in August, 1997. I first met Father Saidi when I was six years old. He is a scholar and a poet, and the kindest, most spiritual person I have ever known. I am very proud to include his chaplet in this book. The greatest compliment I can pay to Father Saidi is to say that he is a priest who has truly lived up to his vocation by helping many people live up to their Faith.

This chaplet may be recited on ordinary Rosary beads.

1. Take your Rosary, bless yourself and kiss the Cross. Look at the Cross and say:

Lord Jesus, we believe in You as You are the Son of Mary and the Son of the Living God, Creator and Redeemer. You came from heaven to earth to save all mankind. You are the Savior of the world. You taught us to pray:

Our Father, who art in heaven, hallowed be Thy name; Thy kingdom come; Thy will be done on earth as it is in heaven. Give us this day our daily bread; and forgive us our trespasses as we forgive those who trespass against us; and lead us not into temptation, but deliver us from evil.

For Thine is the kingdom, the power and the glory, now and forever. Amen.

2. On the first Our Father bead and on all that follow, instead of the Our Father say:

Merciful Jesus, our Redeemer, You said, "ask and you shall receive." We humbly ask You to hear our prayer, forgive us our sins and grant us Your peace and salvation. We praise You now and forever. Amen.

3. On the fifty-three beads of your chaplet say instead of the Hail Mary:

Holy God, Holy Mighty One, Holy Immortal One, have mercy on us.

4. At the end of each decade instead of the Glory be to the Father say:

Most blessed Virgin Mary, Mother of God, intercede for us.

5. At the end of the last decade of the chaplet say:

Most blessed Virgin Mary, Mother of God, intercede for us, for the forgiveness of our sins, peace and eternal salvation from your loving Son, our Lord Jesus Christ, the only Son of the Living God, and we praise you, we bless His name now and forever.

Glory be to the Father, and to the Son, and to the Holy Spirit, as it was in the beginning, is now, and ever shall be, world without end. Amen.

THE ROSARY OF JESUS

This ancient chaplet from centuries ago is becoming very popular today, especially in prayer groups.

The rosary commemorates the 33 years of Jesus' life on earth. It consists of the Apostles' Creed, 33 Our Fathers and 7 Glory Be's. There are seven mysteries to be meditated upon. Each mystery is a different aspect of the life of Jesus.

First Mystery: The Birth of Jesus.
Prayer Intention: For peace in the world.
Meditation and spontaneous prayer.
5 Our Fathers.
O Jesus, be our strength and protection.

Second Mystery: Jesus' love and compassion for the poor and afflicted.
Prayer Intention: For the Holy Father and the bishops.
(Repeat Meditation, Our Fathers and O Jesus.)

Third Mystery: Jesus trusted in His Father and carried out His will.
Prayer Intention: Let us pray for priests, brothers and sisters and for all those who serve God in a particular way.
(Repeat Meditation, Our Fathers and O Jesus.)

The Rosary of Jesus

Fourth Mystery: Jesus willingly came to earth, suffered and died because He loved us so much.

Prayer Intention: Let us pray for families, for parents, and their children.

(Repeat Meditation, Our Fathers and O Jesus.)

Fifth Mystery: Jesus gave up His life as a sacrifice for us.

Prayer Intention: Let us pray that we too may be capable of offering our life for our neighbor.

(Repeat Meditation, Our Fathers and O Jesus.)

Sixth Mystery: The Resurrection of Jesus, His victory over Satan and death.

Prayer Intention: Let us pray that we may eliminate all sin from our lives so that Jesus may live in our hearts.

(Repeat Meditation, Our Fathers and O Jesus.)

Seventh Mystery: The Ascension of Jesus into heaven.

Prayer Intention: Let us pray that the will of God may triumph so that we may be open to the will of God in our lives.

(Repeat Meditation, Our Fathers and O Jesus.)

Meditation: Let us contemplate how Jesus sent the Holy Spirit. Let us pray that the Holy Spirit may descend upon us.

Glory be to the Father 7 times.

The Infant Jesus

CHAPLET OF THE HOLY INFANT JESUS

This devotion owes its origin to the zeal of the Venerable Sister Marguerite of the Blessed Sacrament, a Carmelite religious, who died in the odor of sanctity at Beaune, France, May 26, 1648, aged 27 years.

The Divine Infant revealed to His faithful servant how pleasing to Him is this holy practice. He promised her that He would grant special graces, above all purity of heart and innocence, to all who carried the chaplet on their person and recited it in honor of the mysteries of His Holy Infancy. As a sign of His approval, He showed her these chaplets shining with a supernatural light.

On the medal the following invocation is said:

Divine Infant Jesus, I adore Your Cross, and I accept all the crosses You will be pleased to send me. Adorable Trinity, I offer You for the glory of the Holy Name of God all the adorations of the Sacred Heart of the Holy Infant Jesus.

This Rosary is recited as follows: Our Father three times in honor of the Holy Family; Hail Mary twelve times in honor of the twelve years of our Divine Savior's Infancy.

Before each Our Father say: And the Word was made flesh, and dwelt among us.

Say the same words before the first Hail Mary.

At the end of the chaplet, say:

Holy Infant Jesus, bless and protect us!

The Chaplet of the Holy Infant Jesus

HEART OF THE WORLD
DEVOTION TO THE INFANT JESUS

This chaplet consists of a medal of the Infant Jesus followed by three beads, followed by thirty beads.

1. Say an Act of Contrition.

2. On the beads say thirty times: My little Jesus, I love Thee.

3. Say three times: Mother of Perpetual Help, save us.

Let us pray.

My little Jesus, if it be Thy Holy Will, look upon my poor petition and grant me the favor I so earnestly beg of Thee. In return, I will ever love Thee, Divine Babe, and will do all in my power to make Thee known and loved. Amen.

+ *Imprimatur:* George W. Ahr, Bishop of Trenton, February 22, 1960.

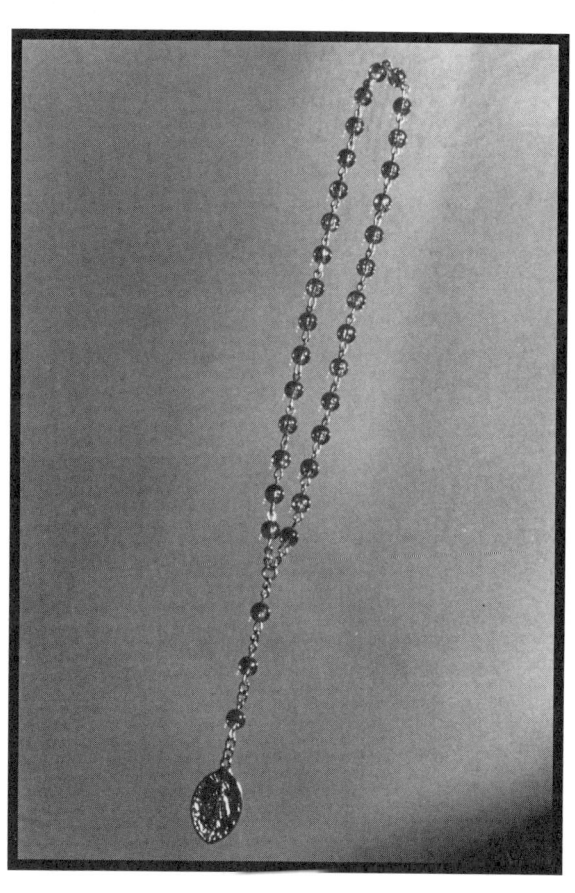

Heart of the World

ROSARY OF THE HOLY WOUNDS

May be said on ordinary prayer beads.

O Jesus, divine Redeemer, have mercy upon us and upon the whole world! Amen.

O powerful God! O Holy God! O Immortal God! Have pity on us and upon the whole world! Amen.

Pardon and mercy, O my Jesus, during these present dangers. Pour on us Thy Most Precious Blood! Amen.

O Eternal Father, be merciful to us through the Blood of Jesus Christ Thy only Son! Be merciful to us, we beseech Thee!

On the small beads say the following:

My Jesus, pardon and mercy, through the merits of Thy Holy Wounds!

On the large beads say:

Eternal Father, I offer Thee the Wounds of Our Lord Jesus Christ to heal the wounds of our souls. *(Repeat this prayer three times.)*

These invocations were taught by Our Lord Himself to Sister Mary Chambon, humble lay sister at Chambery.

Our Lord made the following promises in favor of those who recite this chaplet:

Promises of Our Lord to Sr. Mary Martha

"I will grant all that is asked of Me by the invocation of My HOLY WOUNDS. You must spread the devotion."

"With My WOUNDS and My DIVINE HEART you can obtain everything."

"The sinner who will say: Eternal Father, I offer Thee the WOUNDS of Our Lord Jesus Christ, etc., will obtain conversion."

"The HOLY WOUNDS are the treasures for the souls in Purgatory."

"The CHAPLET OF MERCY is a counterpoise to My justice; it restrains My vengeance."

"At each word that you pronounce of the CHAPLET OF MERCY I allow a drop of My Blood to fall upon the soul of a sinner."

From the brochure: "Sr. M. Martha Chambon and the Holy Wounds of Our Lord."

LITTLE CHAPLET OF THE FIVE WOUNDS OF JESUS CRUCIFIED

I.

O my Lord Jesus Christ, I adore the wound in Thy left foot. I thank Thee for having suffered it for me with so much sorrow and with so much love. I compassionate Thy pain, and that of Thine afflicted Mother. And, by the merit of this sacred wound, I pray Thee to grant me the pardon of my sins, of which I repent with all my heart, because they have offended Thine infinite goodness. O sorrowing Mary, pray to Jesus for me.

Our Father, Hail Mary, Glory be, etc.

By all the wounds which Thou didst bear
With so much love and so much pain,
Oh, let a sinner's prayer
Thy mercy, Lord, obtain!

II.

O my Lord Jesus Christ, I adore the wound in Thy right foot. I thank Thee for having suffered it for me with so much sorrow and with so much love. I compassionate Thy pain, and that of Thine afflicted Mother. And, by the merit of this sacred wound, I pray Thee to give me the strength not to fall into mortal sin for the future, but to persevere in Thy grace unto my death. O sorrowing Mary, pray to Jesus for me.

Our Father, Hail Mary, Glory be, etc.
By all the wounds which Thou didst bear
With so much love and so much pain,
Oh, let a sinner's prayer
Thy mercy, Lord, obtain!

III.

O my Lord Jesus Christ, I adore the wound in Thy left hand. I thank Thee for having suffered it for me with so much sorrow and with so much love. I compassionate Thy pain, and that of Thine afflicted Mother. And, by the merit of this sacred wound, I pray Thee to deliver me from hell, which I have so often deserved, where I could never love Thee more. O sorrowing Mary, pray to Jesus for me.

Our Father, Hail Mary, Glory be, etc.
By all the wounds which Thou didst bear
With so much love and so much pain,
Oh, let a sinner's prayer
Thy mercy, Lord, obtain!

IV.

O my Lord Jesus Christ, I adore the wound in Thy right hand. I thank Thee for having suffered it for me with so much sorrow and with so much love. I compassionate Thy pain, and that of Thine afflicted Mother. And, by the merit of this sacred wound, I pray Thee to give me the glory of paradise, where I shall love Thee perfectly, and with all my strength. O sorrowing Mary, pray to Jesus for me.

Our Father, Hail Mary, Glory be, etc.

By all the wounds which Thou didst bear
With so much love and so much pain,
Oh, let a sinner's prayer
Thy mercy, Lord, obtain!

V.

O my Lord Jesus Christ, I adore the wound in Thy side. I thank Thee for having suffered it for me with so much sorrow and with so much love. I compassionate Thy pain, and that of Thine afflicted Mother. And, by the merit of this sacred wound, I pray Thee to bestow upon me the gift of holy love for Thee, that so I may ever love Thee in this life, and in the other, face to face, for all eternity, in paradise. O sorrowing Mary, pray to Jesus for me.

Our Father, Hail Mary, Glory be, etc.

By all the wounds which Thou didst bear
With so much love and so much pain,
Oh, let a sinner's prayer
Thy mercy, Lord, obtain!

Chaplet of the Five Wounds

CHAPLET OF THE FIVE WOUNDS

(Passionist)

This chaplet contains 5 groups of beads each. On each bead one Glory be is said, and between the groups one Hail Mary in honor of the Sorrowful Virgin. Meanwhile one meditation on the Wounds of Our Lord Jesus Christ. Usually there are medals attached to the beads, or 3 beads added at the beginning of the chaplet. These medals show the Wounds of Christ on one side and Our Lady of Sorrows on the other. They are not required either for blessing or for gaining the indulgences. Ordinarily the beads are so arranged that we meditate first on the Wound on the left foot of Our Lord, then those in the right foot, the left hand, the right hand and finally the Wound in the sacred side.

The first mention of the beads of the Five Wounds is found in a document dating back to 1821. The Platea of Sts. John and Paul, at Rome, relates: "The Most Rev. Fr. General, acting in accordance with our spirit to promote devotion to the Passion of Our Lord, obtained permission to bless the Chaplet of the Five Wounds, at the same time enriching it with indulgences." This chaplet was first approved by a decree of Pius VII dated Jan. 2, 1822.

THE CHAPLET OF THE HOLY FACE

The fourteen beads which form the Chaplet of the Holy Face are to remind us of the fourteen stations on the Way of the Cross.

Recite the following prayer while 1) keeping one's eyes on the picture of the Holy Face of Jesus, or 2) venerating the medal of the Holy Face of Jesus (it shows the Holy Face on one side and a sacred host on the other), or 3) holding one's arms outstretched in the shape of a cross. (This is suggested in the privacy of your home.)

Eternal Father, for my own and the salvation of all men, I offer You the infinite merits of Your beloved Son, Jesus Christ, whose Holy Face unveils to us Your fatherly mercy as well as Your godly presence. It is He who told us: "Who sees Me, sees the Father." Through the sorrowful, immaculate and merciful heart of Mary, Your beloved daughter, the faithful and ever Virgin Spouse of the Holy Spirit and Mother of Your Son, our Lord and Redeemer, I offer You the infinite merits which the Holy Face of Jesus has earned for us. I offer them also through St. Joseph, the faithful manager of all the gifts and favors coming from You, the Father of light and mercy. I also express my thankfulness for the Holy Face of Jesus, our

Mediator, Who protects us against every interior and exterior harm.

Then on each and every one of the fourteen beads, recite the following invocation:

Let the light of Your Holy Face shine on us and in Your mercy save us.

Chaplet or Crown of the Holy Face

THE CHAPLET (OR CROWN)
OF THE HOLY FACE

The purpose of the Crown or Chaplet of the Holy Face is to honor the Five Wounds of Our Lord Jesus Christ, and to ask of God the triumph of His holy Church.

This chaplet is composed of a Cross and thirty-nine beads; of these six are large beads and thirty-three are small. To this chaplet is attached a medal of the Holy Face.

On the Cross, which reminds us of the mystery of our redemption, we begin the chaplet by saying the words:

Incline unto my aid, O God! O Lord, make haste to help me! Glory be to the Father, etc.

The thirty-three small beads represent the thirty-three years of the mortal life of our Divine Lord. The first thirty beads recall to us the thirty years of His hidden life, and are divided into five parts of six beads each, in honor of the senses of touch, hearing, sight, smell and taste of Jesus, and as they were situated principally in His Holy Face, to render reparative homage for all the sufferings which Our Lord has endured in His Face through each of these senses.

Each set of six beads is preceded by a large bead, followed by a Glory be to the Father to recall the sense we wish to honor. The other three beads mark the three years of the public life of Our Lord, and have for their intention to honor all the wounds of His adorable Face; these are also preceded by a large bead, to be followed by a Glory be to the Father for the same intention.

On each large bead say: My Jesus, mercy!

On the small beads say: Arise, O Lord, and let Thy enemies be scattered, and let them that hate Thee fly before Thy Face!

The Glory be to the Father is recited seven times in honor of the Seven Last Words of Jesus upon the Cross, and the Seven Dolors of the Immaculate Virgin.

The chaplet is concluded by saying on the medal:

God, our Protector, look down upon us and cast Thine eyes upon the Face of Thy Christ!

This chaplet was composed by Sister Saint Pierre, a Carmelite of Tours. St. Athanasius relates that the devils, on being asked what verse in the whole Scripture they feared the most, replied: "That with which the sixty-seventh psalm commences: 'Let God arise, and let His enemies be scattered. Let them that hate Him flee from before His Face.'" They added that this always compelled them to take flight.

ROSARY IN HONOR OF
THE SACRED FACE

Most Sacred Face, we call on You until You hear our prayers. You are able to help us wonderfully. Holy God, Mighty God, Holy Immortal God! Have mercy on us and on the whole world! Turn Your Face towards us and we shall be saved!

On the large beads we pray:

Heavenly Father, humbly and fervently we offer You the infinite merits and sufferings of the Sacred Face, His Precious Blood, all the wounds and tears of Jesus, to Your greater Glory, for help in our great need.

On the small beads, instead of the Hail Mary, we pray:
First Decade
O Sacred Face, covered with wounds, have mercy on us who call on You!

Second Decade
O Sacred Face, covered with blood, have mercy on us who call on You!

Third Decade

O Sacred Face, shedding tears with infinite Love, have mercy on us who call on You!

Fourth Decade

O Sacred Face, despised and insulted, have mercy on us who call on You!

Fifth Decade

O Sacred Face, silently bearing the most bitter pain, have mercy on us who call on You!

Let us adore the Sacred Face of Our Lord Jesus Christ, our Savior, whose merits are infinite and whose mercy is fathomless. May He grant us the remission of our sins and true conversion. Let us console His Sacred Face by the purity of our lives, by fearless witness to our Faith and by the depth of our love! Amen.

THE CHAPLET OF THE WAY
OF THE CROSS

This chaplet consists of 15 groups of 3 beads each, between which are medals representing the Stations of the Cross. An additional 6 beads are added as well as a Crucifix.

This chaplet of the Way of the Cross was granted to the Vincentian Order by Popes Pius IX and X. Later it was withdrawn by the Holy Office (1912), since the indulgences can be gained by using the Crucifix alone.

It is somewhat of a misnomer to call this a rosary. To the sick and to others who cannot go to a church to make the Way of the Cross, the Holy See has given the privilege of gaining the indulgences attached to the Way of the Cross by holding in their hand a specially indulgenced Crucifix and saying the prescribed prayers: the Our Father, Hail Mary and Glory be 20 times.

*A Suggested Way of Saying
the Way of the Cross Rosary*

On the Crucifix say the Apostles' Creed.

On each of the following six beads:

1. An Act of Contrition.

2. Prayer to Jesus Christ Crucified:

Behold, O kind and most sweet Jesus, I cast myself on my knees in Your sight and with the most fervent desire of my soul I pray and beg You to impress upon my heart lively sentiments of faith, hope and charity, with true repentance for my sins, and a firm desire of amendment, while with deep affection and grief of soul I ponder within myself and mentally contemplate Your five most precious wounds: having before my eyes that which David spoke in prophecy: "The have pierced My hands and My feet; they have numbered all My bones."

3. Eternal rest grant unto them, O Lord, and let perpetual light shine upon them; and may all the souls of the faithful departed through the mercy of God rest in peace. Amen.

4. Our Father

5. Hail Mary

6. Glory be

For the intentions of the Holy Father: at each medal/station say:

We adore You, O Christ, and we bless You, because by Your Holy Cross You have redeemed the world.

Followed by:

Our Father, Hail Mary, Glory be.

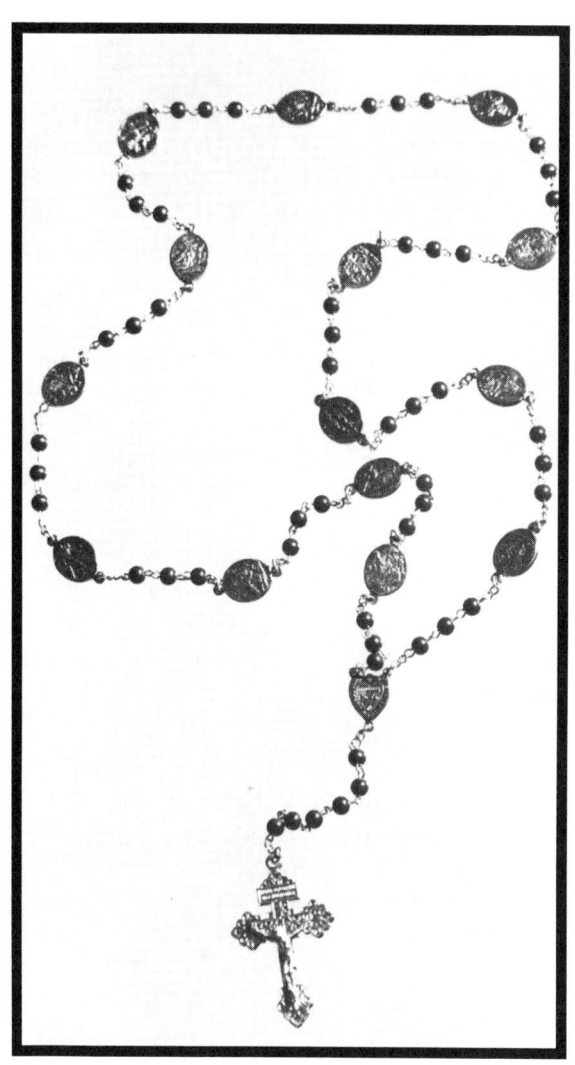

Way of the Cross

THE CROWN OF OUR LORD

*The Crown of Our Lord consists of 33 beads –
3 decades and 3 additional beads commemorat-
ing the 33 years of the earthly life of Our Lord.
There are two methods of reciting this crown.
The first method is as follows: Having made the
Sign of the Cross say:*

V. O God, incline unto my aid.
R. O Lord, make haste to help me.

The Mystery is then announced, e.g.,
Jesus, Who sweat blood for us, etc.

*Then say 1 Hail Mary, 10 Our Fathers and 1
Glory be. These are all to be repeated 3 times.*
*Then add 1 Hail Mary, 3 Our Fathers and
another Hail Mary. The 5 Hail Marys are to
commemorate the Five Holy Wounds.*

*The second method of reciting the Crown con-
sists of meditating on an event from the life or
Passion of Our Lord while saying the prescribed
Our Father or Hail Mary.*

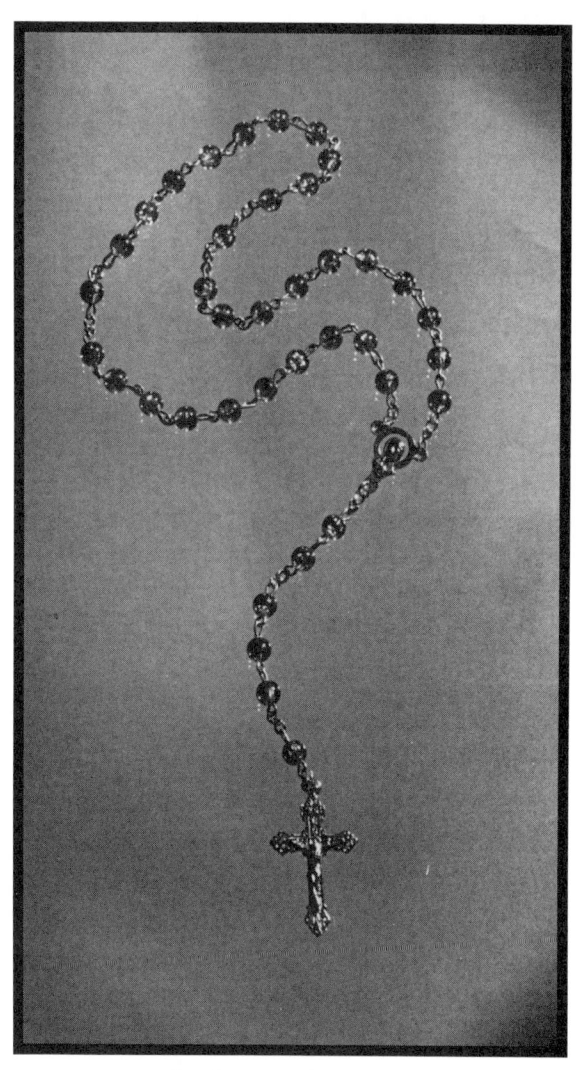

The Crown of Our Lord

CHAPLET TO OBTAIN
A GREAT CONFIDENCE

The ordinary prayer beads may be used. On the large beads repeat the prayer See where, etc. *(below). On the small beads repeat the ejaculation* Sacred Heart of Jesus, I trust in Thee!

Our Lord has for some time deigned to work many wonders through the invocation:

Sacred Heart of Jesus, I trust in Thee!

See where Thy boundless Love has reached, my loving Jesus! Thou of Thy Flesh and Precious Blood hast made ready for me a banquet whereby to give me all Thyself. Who drove Thee to this excess of love for me? Thy Heart, Thy loving Heart! O adorable Heart of Jesus, burning furnace of Divine Love! Within Thy Sacred Wounds take Thou my soul, in order that, in that school of charity, I may learn to love that God Who hast given me such wondrous proofs of His great love. Amen.

Sacred Heart of Jesus, etc. *(ten times).*

BEADS OF THE SACRED HEART
by Father Croiset, S.J.

As there is nothing so ingenious as love, some of the saints in their great eagerness to make, each day, numerous acts of their favorite virtues according to the various inspirations of grace, have invented several kinds of chaplets composed of acts of these virtues. After their example, the Beads of the Sacred Heart has been formed. It is composed of five large beads and thirty-three small ones in honor of the thirty-three years Our Lord spent on earth.

Instead of the Creed, say the following prayer:

Anima Christi
Soul of Christ, be my sanctification.
Body of Christ, be my salvation.
Blood of Christ, fill all my veins.
Water from Christ's side, wash out my
    stains.
Passion of Christ, my comfort be.
O good Jesus, listen to me.
In Thy wounds I fain would hide,
Ne'er to be parted from Thy side.
Guard me should the foe assail me.
Call me when my life shall fail me.
Bid me come to Thee above,
With Thy saints to sing Thy love,
World without end. Amen.

Before each large bead say:
Jesus most meek, make my heart like unto Thine.

On each large bead say:
We adore Thee, O Jesus, who hast been afflicted in the Garden of Gethsemane and who still in our time art outraged in the Blessed Sacrament by the impious conduct of men. O most amiable Savior, we recognize that Thou alone are Holy, Thou alone art Lord, Thou alone art Most High.

On each small bead say:
I adore Thee, O most Sacred Heart of Jesus! Inflame my heart with the Divine Love with which Thine own is all on fire!

At the end of the beads say an Our Father and a Hail Mary, and the following prayer:
O Lord Jesus Christ, Who by an ineffable miracle of love hast deigned to give Thy Heart to men to serve as their nourishment, in order thereby to gain their hearts, graciously hear our humble prayers, and pardon us for the sins of which we confess ourselves guilty before Thee. Cast an eye of compassion and mercy upon those towards whom Thou dost condescend to direct the affections of Thine amiable Heart. And since we desire to honor Thee in the adorable Mystery of the Altar to the utmost of our

power and to render Thee most pleasing homage, and for that intention, weep for and detest from the bottom of our hearts all the outrages, contempt, mockery, sacrileges, and other acts of impiety which ungrateful men in every part of the world have committed against Thee, enkindle therefore in our hearts this divine love with which Thine own is inflamed, and inspire us with sentiments like unto Thine, in order that we may be able worthily to praise for all eternity the love with which this Sacred Heart burns for us. This our prayer to Thee who livest and reignest with the Father, in the unity of the Holy Spirit forever and ever. Amen.

BEADS OF THE SACRED HEART
(recited on regular beads)

On the Cross of the Rosary Beads say:
   Angel of God, my guardian dear,
   To whom God's love commits me here,
   Ever this day be at my side,
   To light and guard, to rule and guide.

On the first large bead say:
   O Eternal Father, I offer Thee the Blood,
Passion and death of Our Lord Jesus Christ
and the sorrows of our Blessed Lady and St.
Joseph in reparation for my sins, in suffrage
for the souls in Purgatory, for the wants of
our Holy Church, and for the conversion of
sinners.

On the three small beads say:
   My God, I believe in Thee.
   My God, I hope in Thee.
   My God, I love Thee with my whole
heart, and for Thy sake I love my neighbor
as myself.

On each of the large beads of the five decades say:
   Jesus, meek and humble of heart, make
my heart like unto Thine.
   O Mary conceived without sin, pray for
me.

On each of the small beads of the five decades say:

Sweetest Heart of Jesus, I implore, that I may love Thee more and more.

Sweet Heart of Mary, be thou my salvation.

In conclusion say:

Jesus, Mary and Joseph, I give you my heart and my soul.

Jesus, Mary and Joseph, assist me now and in my last agony.

Jesus, Mary and Joseph, may I breathe forth my soul in peace with you.

INDULGENCED CHAPLET OF THE SACRED HEART OF JESUS

(With Acts of Thanksgiving, Contrition and Love)

V. Incline unto my aid, O God!
R. O Lord, make haste to help me!

1. Most loving Jesus! My heart leaps for joy in thinking of Thy loving Sacred Heart, all tenderness and sweetness for sinful man; and with trust unbounded, it never doubts Thy ready welcome. Ah me! My sins! How many and how great! With Peter and Magdalen, in tears, I bewail and abhor them, because they are an offense to Thee, my sole and chief good. Grant me, O grant me pardon for them all! O may I die, I beseech Thee, by Thy loving Heart, may I die rather than offend Thee; and may I live only to correspond to Thy love!

Say the Our Father once, the Glory be to the Father five times, and then:
    O sweetest Heart of Jesus, I implore that I may ever love Thee more and more!

2. My Jesus! I bless Thy most humble Heart, and I give thanks to Thee, Who, in making it my model, not only dost urge me

with such pressing to imitate it, but, at the cost of so many humiliations, dost Thyself stoop to point me out the path and smooth for me the way to follow Thee. Foolish and ungrateful that I am, how have I wandered far away from Thee! Mercy, my Jesus, mercy! Away hateful pride and love of worldly honor! With lowly heart I wish to follow Thee, my Jesus, through humiliations and the Cross, and thus to gain peace and salvation. Only be Thou at hand to strengthen me, and I will ever bless Thy Sacred Heart!

Our Father once, Glory be to the Father five times, and then:

O sweetest Heart of Jesus, etc.

3. My Jesus! I marvel at Thy most patient Heart, and I thank Thee for all those wondrous examples of unwearied patience which Thou didst leave me to guide me on my way. It grieves me that I have still to reproach myself with my extravagant delicacy, shrinking from the slightest pain. O pour then into my heart, dear Jesus, eager and enduring love of suffering and of the Cross, of mortification and of penance, that following Thee to Calvary, I may with Thee attain the joys of paradise!

Our Father once, Glory be to the Father five times.

O sweetest Heart of Jesus, etc.

4. Dear Jesus! At the sight of Thy most gentle Heart, I shudder to see how unlike mine is to Thine, since at a shadow, at a look, at a word of opposition, I fret and grieve. O then, pardon my excesses, and give me grace that in every contradiction I may follow the example of Thy unchangeable meekness, and so enjoy an everlasting holy peace.!

Our Father once, Glory be to the Father five times.

O sweetest Heart of Jesus, etc.

5. Sing praise to Jesus for His most generous Heart, the Conqueror of death and hell; yet never wilt thou reach its due with all thy praise. More than ever am I confounded looking upon my cowardly heart, which through human respect dreads even a passing word. Courage, my soul! It shall be so with thee no more. My Jesus, I pray Thee for such strength that, fighting and conquering on earth, I may one day rejoice triumphantly with Thee in heaven.

Our Father once, Glory be to the Father five times.

O sweetest Heart of Jesus, etc.

Let us turn to Mary, consecrating ourselves to her more and more, and trusting in her maternal Heart, let us say to her:

By the gracious gifts of thy sweetest Heart, obtain for me, great Mother of my God and my Mother Mary, a true and lasting devotion to the Sacred Heart of Jesus, thy well-beloved Son, that, united in every thought and affection with that Heart, I may fulfill all the duties of my state in life with ready heart, serving my Jesus ever more, but especially on this day.

V. Heart of Jesus, burning with love for us,
R. Inflame our hearts with love of Thee.

Let us pray

Lord, we beseech Thee, let Thy Holy Spirit kindle in our hearts that fire of charity which Our Lord Jesus Christ, Thy Son, sent forth from His inmost Heart upon this earth, and willed that it should burn with vehemence. Who liveth and reigneth with Thee, in the unity of the same Holy Spirit, God for ever and ever. Amen.

THE ROSARY OF THE SACRED HEART

The chaplet consists of 33 small beads, 6 large beads, a Crucifix and a Sacred Heart medal.

On the Crucifix say the Anima Christi:
Soul of Christ, sanctify me!.
Body of Christ, save me!
Blood of Christ, inebriate me!
Water from the side of Christ, wash me!
Passion of Christ, strengthen me!
O good Jesus, hear me!
Within Thy wounds hide me!
Let me not be separated from Thee!
From the evil enemy defend me!
In the hour of death call me and bid me come over to Thee, that with Thy saints I may praise Thee forever and ever. Amen

On the large beads say:
O sweetest Heart of Jesus, I implore that I may ever love Thee more and more!

On the small beads say:
Sweet Heart of Jesus, be my love!

At the end of each decade say:
Sweet Heart of Mary, be my salvation!

At the conclusion say:
May the heart of Jesus in the Most Blessed Sacrament be blessed, adored and loved with grateful affection at every moment in all the tabernacles of the world, even to the end of time!

The Rosary of the Sacred Heart

CHAPLET OF THE TWO HEARTS

There are 20 beads in 5 sets, each consisting of 1 Our Father and 3 Hail Marys.

These are the meditations for the five sets:

1. *In honor of the Sacred Heart of Jesus.*
2. *In honor of the Immaculate Heart of Mary.*
3. *The Passion of Our Lord.*
4. *The Sorrows of Mary.*
5. *In atonement to the Hearts of Jesus and Mary.*

At the end on the medal say the prayer to the United Hearts of Jesus and Mary:

O United Hearts of Jesus and Mary, You are all grace, all mercy, all love. Let my heart be joined to Yours, so that my every need is present in Your United Hearts. Most especially, shed Your grace upon this particular need *(mention your need)*. Help me to recognize and accept Your loving will in my life. Amen.

For more information on this chaplet, please contact:
Mary's House of Prayer
6779 Broadview Road
Seven Hills, Ohio 44131 USA

CHAPLET OF THE PRECIOUS BLOOD

This devotion consists of seven mysteries in which we meditate on the seven principal sheddings of the Most Precious Blood of Jesus. The Our Father without the Hail Mary is said five times after each mystery except the last, when it is said three times – in all, thirty-three times in honor of the thirty-three years of Our Lord's life on earth.

V. O God, come to my assistance!
R. Lord, make haste to help me!
V. Glory be to the Father, etc.
R. As it was in the beginning, etc.

First Mystery

Jesus shed His Blood in the Circumcision. Let us ask for chastity of soul and body.

Our Father five times, Glory be to the Father once.

V. We pray you, Lord, help your servants!
R. Whom You have redeemed with Your Precious Blood!

(This invocation to the Precious Blood is said after the Our Father and Glory be of each mystery.)

Second Mystery

Jesus shed His Blood in the Agony while praying in the Garden of Olives. Let us ask for the spirit of prayer.

Third Mystery

Jesus shed His Blood in the Scourging at the Pillar. Let us ask for patience and self control.

Fourth Mystery

Jesus shed His Blood in the Crowning with Thorns. Let us ask for humility to atone for pride.

Fifth Mystery

Jesus shed His Blood while carrying His Cross to Calvary. Let us ask for acceptance of our daily crosses.

Sixth Mystery

Jesus shed His Blood in the terrible Crucifixion. Let us ask for contrition.

Seventh Mystery

Jesus shed Blood and water from His side pierced by the Lance. Let us ask for perseverance.

The Chaplet of the Precious Blood

CHAPLET OF THE HOLY NAME OF JESUS

Begin with the Act of Contrition. On the large bead say:

V. Incline unto my aid, O God.

R. O Lord, make haste to help me.

First Decade – Lord, Thou hast said: "Ask and you shall receive, seek and you shall find, knock and it shall be opened unto you." I seek, I knock, I ask this favor *(name it)*.

Repeat Incline unto my aid, etc., *ten times.*

Second Decade – "Amen, I say unto you, if you ask the Father anything in My Name it shall be given unto you." It is of the Father and in Thy Name, Lord, I ask this favor.

Repeat Incline unto my aid, etc., *ten times.*

Third Decade – Lord, Thou hast said, "Heaven and earth shall pass away, but My word shall not pass away." Thou wilt grant me this favor because Thou hast said it and Thy word is true.

Repeat Incline unto my aid, etc., *ten times.*

Quid ad te? Tu Me sequere.

What is it to thee? Do thou follow Me.

BYZANTINE ROSARY
THE JESUS PRAYER

This dates back to the 7th century when, according to tradition, a saint had an apparition recommending this form of prayer. In Russia the Rosary is called *"Chotki."* It is usually made of wool in which there are 100 knots, with a large knot at each decade. St. Basil the Great used a Rosary of this type.

The customary prayer in the "Chotki" is an adaptation of the humble prayer of the publican who cried out: "O God, have mercy on me, a sinner." *(Luke 18:13-14)* The Lord Jesus said that he went out from his prayer "justified."

Early Christians adopted this prayer for their own use, and added to it the *Prayer of Jesus* or *The Jesus Prayer* and have several variations of it:

Lord Jesus Christ have mercy on me.
or
Lord Jesus Christ, Son of God, have mercy on me.
or
Lord Jesus Christ, by the prayers of Our Lady, have mercy on me.

The Rosary Begins:

O God, cleanse me, a sinner. *(3 times)*

O heavenly King, Paraclete, Spirit of Truth, Who is present everywhere and permeates all things, Treasury of blessings and Giver of life, come and dwell within us. Purify us from every fault and save our souls, O gracious Lord.

Holy God, Holy Mighty One, Holy Immortal One, have mercy on us. *(3 times)*

Glory be to the Father, and to the Son, and to the Holy Spirit, now and always and forever and ever. Amen.

O Holy Trinity, have mercy on us.

Lord, forgive us our sins.

Most holy God, pardon our transgressions.

Do You who are holy visit us and heal our infirmities for Your name's sake.

Lord, have mercy on us. *(3 times)*

Glory be to the Father, etc.

Our Father, who art in heaven, hallowed by Thy name. The kingdom come, Thy will be done on earth, as it is in heaven. Give us this day our daily bread. And forgive us our trespasses, as we forgive those who trespass against us, and lead us not into temptation, but deliver us from evil, for Thine is the Kingdom, and the Power, and the Glory of the Father and of the Son and of the Holy Spirit, now and always, and forever and ever. Amen.

Come let us bow down to our King and God.
Come let us bow down and adore our King
and God.
Come let us bow down and adore Christ
Himself. Our King and God.

Recite the 50th Psalm and the Creed.

Recite the Prayer of Jesus (100 times).

Conclusion

It is indeed proper to bless you, Mother of
God, the eternally blessed and completely
spotless one and the Mother of our God.
Higher in honor than the Cherubim and incomparably more glorious than the Seraphim, who without harm to your virginity
gave birth to the Word of God.

You do we extol, true Mother of God.

Glory be to the Father, and to the Son, and
to the Holy Spirit, now and always and forever and ever. Amen.

Lord, have mercy. Lord, have mercy. Lord,
have mercy.

By the prayers of our holy fathers, O Lord
Jesus Christ, our God, have mercy on us.

Byzantine Rosary

RUSSIAN ROSARY
(A slightly different version of the Byzantine Rosary)

The Eastern rite rosary dates back to the 7th century, when according to tradition, a saint had an apparition recommending this form of prayer. In Russia the rosary is called "Chotki." It is usually made of wool in which there are 100 knots with an extra knot between each ten. At the end is a Cross also made of knots. St. Basil the Great used a rosary very similar to the type now used.

The customary prayer used is the ejaculation of the publican, who stood at the back of the Temple and said: "Lord have mercy on me, a sinner." Our Lord says he went out justified, thus indirectly recommending this prayer. The Russians call this prayer the prayer of Jesus and have several variations of it:

Lord Jesus Christ, Son of God, have mercy on us.

Lord Jesus Christ, Son of God, have mercy on me, a sinner.

Lord Jesus Christ, by the prayers of Our Lady, have mercy on us.

Sometimes they also use:

Most holy Lady, Mother of God, pray for us sinners.

The Rosary Begins:

O God, cleanse me, a sinner. *(3 times)*

O heavenly King, Paraclete, Spirit of Truth, Who art present everywhere and dost permeate all things, Treasury of blessings and Giver of life, come and take up Thy dwelling within us. Purify us from every stain and save our souls, O gracious Lord.

Holy God, Holy Mighty One, Holy Deathless One, have mercy on us. *(3 times)*

Glory be to the Father, and to the Son, and to the Holy Ghost, as it was in the beginning, is now, and ever shall be forever. Amen.

O Holy Trinity, have mercy on us.

Lord, forgive us our sins.

Most holy God, pardon our transgressions.

Do Thou who art holy visit us and heal our infirmities for Thy name's sake.

Lord, have mercy on us. *(3 times)*

Glory be to the Father, etc.

Our Father, etc.

Come let us bow down to our Lord God.

Come let us bow down and adore our Lord God.

Come let us bow down and adore Christ Himself, Our Lord and God.

50th Psalm, Miserere, or 129th, De Profundis.

Credo. I believe in God, etc.
Prayer of Jesus (100 times).
It is indeed proper to bless thee, Mother of God, the eternally blessed and completely sinless one and the Mother of our God. Higher in honor than the Cherubim and incomparably more glorious than the Seraphim, who without harm to thy virginity didst give birth to the Word of God. Thee we extol, true Mother of God.

Glory be to the Father, and to the Son, and to the Holy Ghost, now and ever and unto ages of ages.
Lord, have mercy. Lord, have mercy. Lord, have mercy.

By the prayers of our holy fathers, Lord, have mercy on us.

HOLY SPIRIT ROSARY

Meditations: The First Mystery
Let us honor the Holy Spirit.

Let us adore Him, the substantial Love which proceeds from the Father and the Son, uniting Them in an eternal and infinite Love.

The Second Mystery
Let us honor the Holy Spirit.

Let us adore Him in the Immaculate Conception of Mary, sanctifying her from the very first instant with a plenitude of grace.

The Third Mystery
Let us honor the Holy Spirit.

Let us adore Him in His operation in the Blessed Virgin Mary at the Incarnation of the Word, the Son of God by His Divine Nature, and the Son of Mary by His Humanity.

The Fourth Mystery
Let us honor the action of the Holy Spirit.

Let us adore Him in His coming to our Holy Mother, the Church, on the glorious Sunday of Pentecost in the Cenacle.

The Fifth Mystery
Let us honor the action of the Holy Spirit.
Let us adore Him abiding forever in the Church and faithfully assisting her, according to His Divine promise, till the end of time.

Directions for using the Holy Spirit beads:

Come Holy Spirit, sweet Guest of my Soul.

Live in me so that I may ever live in Thee!

On the two beads:

Father, Father, send us the promised Paraclete, through Jesus Christ our Lord! Amen.

On each of the seven beads:

Come, Holy Spirit, fill the hearts of Your faithful and enkindle in them the fire of Your Love!

At the end of each section:

Send forth Your Spirit and they shall be recreated; and You shall renew the face of the earth.

O God, Who by the light of the Holy Spirit instructs the hearts of the faithful, give us, by the same Holy Spirit, a love and relish for what is right and just, and a constant enjoyment in His consolation. Through Christ our Lord. Amen.

At the end say the Hail, Holy Queen.

LITTLE CHAPLET OF THE HOLY GHOST

Come, Holy Ghost, enlighten my mind!
Come, inflame my heart!

1. *Take your beads (the Blessed Virgin Rosary) and recite the Apostles' Creed.*
2. *After the Creed, very slowly and devoutly say the Glory be to the Father.*
3. *Then say the Our Father.*
4. *Now, very fervently, say this ejaculation:*

Father, Father, send us the promised Paraclete, through Jesus Christ our Lord. Amen.

5. *Now on each bead, instead of the Hail Mary say with a burning heart:*

Come, Holy Spirit, fill the hearts of Thy faithful and kindle in them the fire of Thy love!

6. *After the tenth bead recite the following official prayer:*

Send forth Thy Spirit and they shall be created. And Thou shalt renew the face of the earth! Let us pray.

O God, Who didst instruct the hearts of Thy faithful by the light of the Holy Spirit, grant us by the same Spirit to be truly wise and evermore to rejoice in His consolation. Through Christ our Lord. Amen.

7. *Then recite the second decade and all the others in the same way as explained. (Beginning at No. 3, Our Father.)*

8. *After the seventh and last decade, recite the Hail, Holy Queen in honor of the Blessed Virgin, our Heavenly Queen, who presided in the Cenacle on the great Sunday of Pentecost.*

A few short reflections may be made on seven glorious mysteries relating to seven wonderful operations of the Paraclete. These meditations should be made briefly between every ten beads.

The First Mystery: Let us honor the Holy Ghost and adore Him Who is Love Substantial, proceeding from the Father and the Son, and uniting them in an infinite and eternal Charity.

The Second Mystery: Let us honor the operation of the Holy Ghost and adore Him in the Immaculate Conception of Mary, sanctifying her from the first moment with the plenitude of grace.

The Third Mystery: Let us honor the operation of the Holy Ghost and adore Him as He fecundates the Virgin Mary in the Incarnation of the Word, the Son of God by His Divine nature and the Son of the Virgin by the flesh.

The Fourth Mystery: Let us honor the operation of the Holy Ghost and adore Him giving birth to the Church on the glorious day of Pentecost in the Cenacle.

The Fifth Mystery: Let us honor the operation of the Holy Ghost and adore Him dwelling in the Church and assisting her faithfully according to the Divine promise, even to the consummation of the world.

The Sixth Mystery: Let us honor the wonderful operation of the Holy Ghost creating within the Church that other Christ, the Priest, and conferring the plenitude of the Priesthood on the Bishops.

The Seventh Mystery: Let us honor the operation of the Holy Ghost and adore Him in the heroic virtue of the saints in the Church, that hidden and marvelous work of the "Adorable Sanctifier."

Practices

Recite the Little Chaplet of the Holy Ghost often, very often, even every day.

Recite it especially on Sundays.

When some important decision must be taken, at certain grave moments, and when special spiritual help is needed.

Every day during recollections and retreats.

As a preparation for the feast of Pentecost. This day witnessed the birth of the Bride of Christ.

This wonderful and simple chaplet must become very familiar to everyone and one of our great Catholic devotions. We must have enlightened piety. The Blessed Virgin, Queen of Doctors and of the Cenacle, will bless you. You will thus win her Heart, "Full of Grace," for she is the masterpiece of the Holy Spirit's operation. In your devotions you should always keep in mind the essential. The first of all devotions must be to the Blessed Trinity, and therefore also to the Holy Spirit.

Father Mateo, SS.CC.

CHAPLET OF THE HOLY SPIRIT

The Chaplet of the Holy Spirit was composed in 1892 by a Franciscan Capuchin missionary of the English province in order to give the faithful an easy means of honoring the Holy Ghost. It was approved by Pope Leo XIII in 1902. It is intended to be in regard to the Holy Ghost what the Dominican Rosary is in regard to the Blessed Virgin.

This Rosary consists of five groups of seven beads each. Before and after each group there are two large beads, that is twelve large beads in all. In addition there are three small beads at the beginning. On these three beads one makes the Sign of the Cross, recites an Act of Contrition and the hymn, Come, Holy Ghost.

In each group, the Glory be to the Father is said on the seven small beads, an Our Father and a Hail Mary on the two large beads. On the remaining two large beads are said the Apostles' Creed and an Our Father and Hail Mary for the intention of the Holy Father.

There is a mystery for each of the five groups; the number five commemorates the Five Wounds of Jesus which are the fountains of grace which the Holy Ghost imparts to all men. The reflections suggested are as follows:

The First Mystery
*By the Holy Ghost is Jesus conceived
of the Blessed Virgin Mary.*

The Meditation: "The Holy Ghost shall come upon thee, and the Power of the Most High shall overshadow thee: and therefore also the holy which shall be born of thee shall be called the Son of God." *(Luke 1:35).*

The Practice: Diligently implore the aid of the Divine Spirit, and Mary's intercession, to imitate the virtues of Jesus Christ, Who is the Model of virtues, so that you may be made conformable to the image of the Son of God.

The Second Mystery
The Spirit of the Lord rested upon Jesus.

The Meditation: "Jesus, being baptized, forthwith came out of the water: and lo! the heavens were opened to Him, and He saw the Spirit of God descending as a dove, and coming upon Him." *(Matthew 3:16).*

The Practice: Hold in the highest esteem the priceless gift of sanctifying grace, infused into your soul by the Holy Ghost in Baptism. Keep the promises to which you then pledged yourself. Increase, by constant practice, Faith, Hope and Charity. Ever live as becometh children of God and members of God's true Church, so as to obtain, hereafter, the inheritance of heaven.

The Third Mystery
By the Spirit is Jesus led into the desert.

The Meditation: "Jesus being full of the Holy Ghost, returned from the Jordan, and was led by the Spirit into the desert for the space of forty days; and was tempted by the devil." *(Luke 4:1, 2).*

The Practice: Be ever grateful for the sevenfold gift of the Holy Ghost bestowed upon you in Confirmation, for the spirit of wisdom and understanding, of counsel and fortitude, of knowledge and piety, and of the fear of the Lord. Faithfully yield to His Divine guidance, so that, in all the trials and temptations of life, you may act manfully, as becometh a perfect Christian and valiant soldier of Jesus Christ.

The Fourth Mystery
The Holy Ghost in the Church.

The Meditation: "Suddenly there came a sound from heaven as of a mighty wind coming, and it filled the whole house where they were sitting…and they were all filled with the Holy Ghost, and began to speak… the wonderful works of God." *(Acts 11:2, 4, 11).*

The Practice: Thank God for having made you a child of His Church which is ever animated and directed by the Divine Spirit, sent into this world for that purpose on the

day of Pentecost. Hear and obey the Holy
See, the infallible mouthpiece of the Holy
Ghost, and the Church, the pillar and
ground of truth. Uphold her doctrines, seek
her interests, defend her rights.

The Fifth Mystery
The Holy Ghost in the soul of the just man.

The Meditation: "Know you not that your
members are the temple of the Holy Ghost,
Who is in you?" *(I Cor. 6:19).*

"Extinguish not the Spirit." *(I Thess. 5:19).*

"And grieve not the Holy Spirit of God
whereby you are sealed unto the day of
redemption." *(Eph. 4:30).*

The Practice: Be ever mindful of the Holy
Ghost Who is within you, and carefully cul-
tivate purity of soul and body. Faithfully
obey His Divine inspirations so that you
may bring forth the Fruits of the Spirit –
Charity, Joy, Peace, Patience, Benignity,
Goodness, Longsuffering, Mildness, Faith,
Modesty, Continency, and Chastity.

*Conclude with the Apostles' Creed as a profes-
sion of faith.*

*Say finally one Our Father, Hail Mary and
Glory be to the Father for the intentions of the
Sovereign Pontiff.*

CHAPLET OF FAITH

On each decade of the rosary pray:
On the large bead: the Apostle's Creed.
On the ten small beads: Jesus, Mary, I love you, save souls, save the consecrated.
At the end, 5 times: Hail Holy Queen.

THE APOSTLES CHAPLET

This chaplet was composed by Mr. Roscoe Parkerson, a successful businessman from Louisiana. Mr. Parkerson has always been a great admirer of Pope John Paul II and wanted to show what he felt was "the Pope's great leadership on earth to all people, and that he is Jesus' present Apostle of the Church." Mr. Parkerson was given a copy of My Treasury of Chaplets, and after reading it he felt it showed him the way to express his great love and admiration for Pope John Paul II.

Mr. Parkerson sent the completed chaplet to the Holy Father on the occasion of his Fiftieth Anniversary in the priesthood. He was granted an audience and received the Holy Father's Apostolic Blessing.

The purpose of the Apostles Chaplet is to honor the twelve Apostles and Pope John Paul II on the celebration of his Fiftieth Ecclesiastical Birthday.

The chaplet is composed of four medals and twelve ruby beads. The twelve beads represent the twelve Apostles and the red color of the rubies signifies the blood of Christ that was shed for all mankind.

Start saying the chaplet on the medal of Pope John Paul II. Offer up a prayer of your choosing to God to give our Holy Father strength in his endeavors and to keep him safe from his enemies.

First ruby bead: recite the Apostles Creed.

On the medal of St. Peter, the first Pope, say a prayer of your choosing asking St. Peter for assistance in obtaining your petition.

Ten ruby beads: say a Hail Mary on each bead.

On the medal of Jesus Christ, the Son of God, say a prayer of your choosing giving thanks to God for blessings He has bestowed on you.

Last ruby bead: say the Our Father.

The medal of St. Peter's crucifix with the Holy Spirit ascending into Heaven ends the chaplet prayers. Say a Glory be to the Father on this medal.

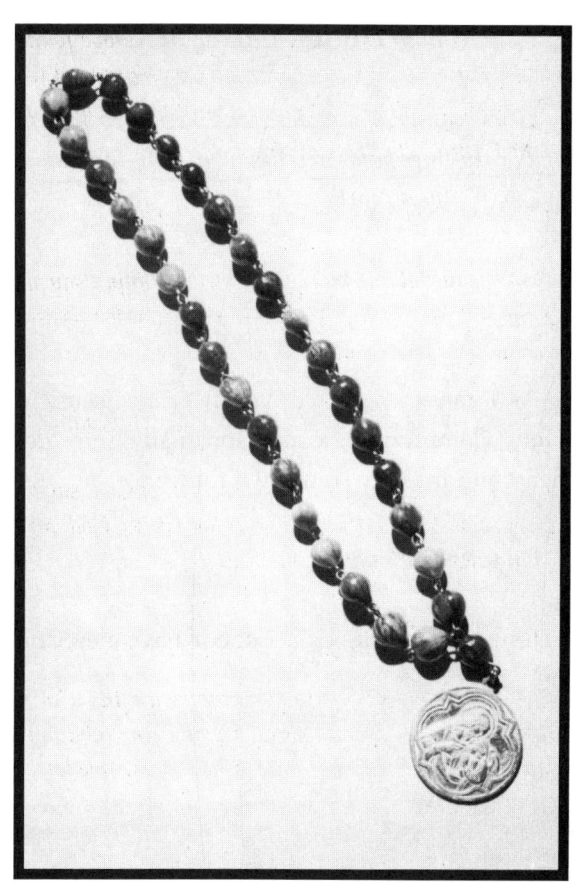

The Blessed Sacrament Beads

BLESSED SACRAMENT BEADS

These consist of a medal of the Blessed Sacrament and thirty-three beads, recalling the thirty-three years of Christ's life on earth.

On the medal one makes a spiritual communion as follows:

As I cannot now receive Thee, my Jesus, in Holy Communion, come spiritually into my heart and make it Thine own forever!

On each bead say:

Jesus in the Blessed Sacrament, have mercy on us!

CHAPLET BEFORE COMMUNION

First Decade:

O My God, Thou art goodness itself, and I am not worthy to receive Thee. My soul thirsts for Thee. Thou art its joy and salvation. O grant that I may be with Thee for all eternity. Come, my Jesus; come, my Love! Come and Thyself prepare my heart.

Second Decade: (Ten times)

Lord, I am not worthy that Thou shouldst enter into my heart; say only the word and I shall be healed.

("Come," etc., as above.)

Third Decade:

As the hart pants after the fountain of living waters, so my heart pants for Thee, my God.

("Come," etc., as above.)

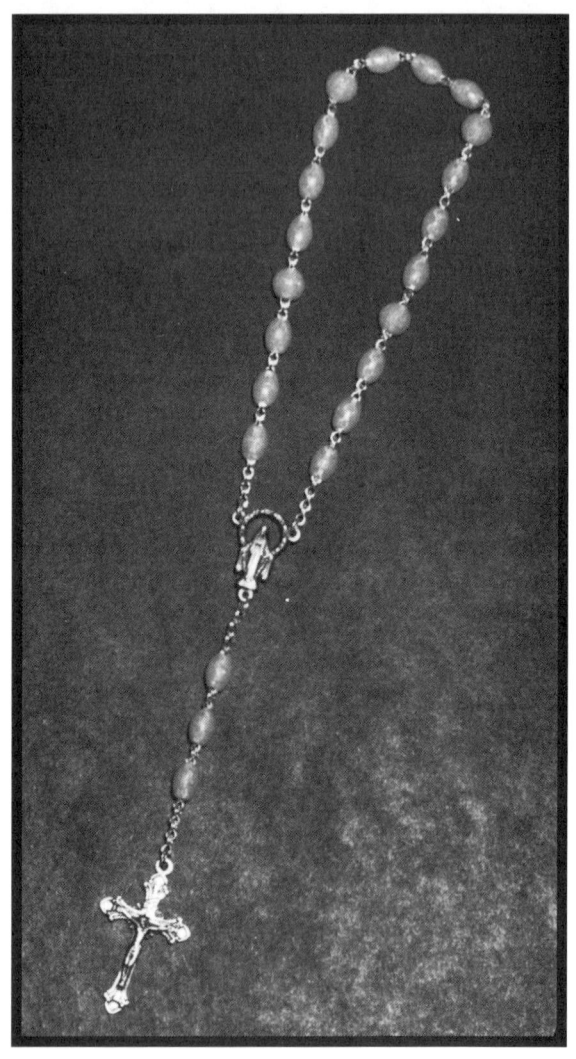

Holy Communion Chaplet

THE HOLY COMMUNION CHAPLET

An Act of Faith

O My God, I firmly believe that Thou art one God in three Divine Persons, Father, Son and Holy Spirit; I believe that Thy Divine Son became man, and died for our sins, and that He will come to judge the living and the dead. I believe these and all the truths which the Holy Catholic Church teaches because Thou hast revealed them, Who canst neither deceive nor be deceived.

An Act of Hope

O My God, relying on Thy almighty power and infinite mercy and promises, I hope to obtain pardon of my sins, the help of Thy grace, and life everlasting, through the merits of Jesus Christ, my Lord and Redeemer.

An Act of Charity

O My God, I love Thee above all things, with my whole heart and soul, because Thou art all-good and worthy of all love. I love my neighbor as myself for the love of Thee. I forgive all who have injured me, and ask pardon of all whom I have injured.

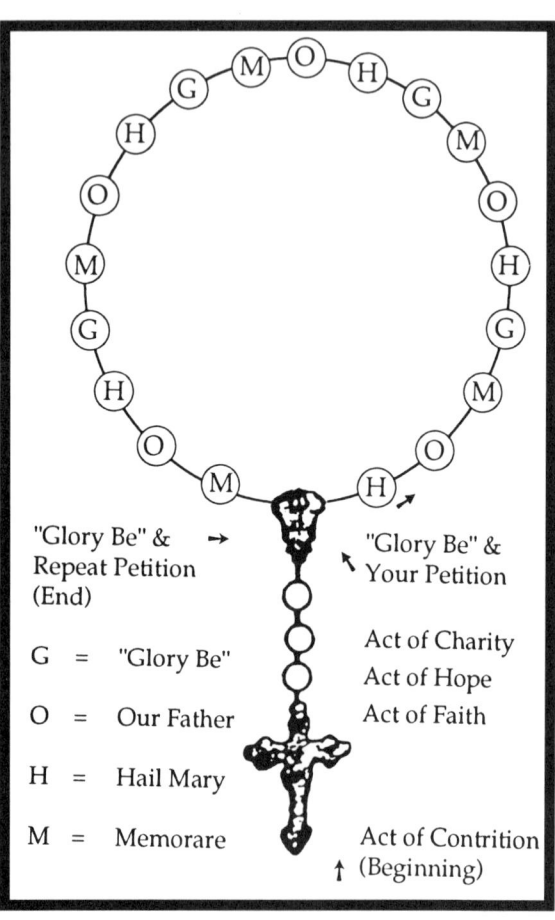

"Glory Be" & → Repeat Petition (End)

G = "Glory Be"

O = Our Father

H = Hail Mary

M = Memorare

"Glory Be" & Your Petition

Act of Charity
Act of Hope
Act of Faith

Act of Contrition
↑ (Beginning)

THE HOLY ROSARY

The Memorare

Remember, O most gracious Virgin Mary, that never was it known that anyone who fled to your protection, implored your help, or sought your intercession, was left unaided. Inspired with this confidence, I fly to you, O Virgin of virgins, my Mother! To you I come; before you I stand, sinful and sorrowful. O Mother of the Word Incarnate, despise not my petitions, but, in your mercy, hear and answer me. Amen.

THE ROSARY OF THE
MOST BLESSED VIRGIN

The word Rosary comes from the Latin word *Rosarium,* a rose garden. The Rosary is a garden filled with lovingly repeated invocations to Our Lady, God the Father and the Blessed Trinity.

The Rosary of Our Lady consists of fifteen decades dedicated to fifteen mysteries in the lives of Jesus and Mary.

It is customary to recite one third of the Rosary daily *(five decades).* On Monday and Thursday the Joyful Mysteries are said; on Tuesday and Friday the Sorrowful Mysteries; and on Wednesday, Saturday and Sunday the Glorious Mysteries.)

It is piously believed that the Rosary was given to St. Dominic by Our Lady while he was combating the Albigensian heresy in the south of France, early in the thirteenth century. It is also believed that the Rosary was in use long before that time as "a poor man's Psalter," the 15O Hail Marys taking the place of the 15O Psalms.

Whatever its origin, the Rosary has proved to be a powerful weapon against evil, and as Pope Leo XIII declared, the best and most fruitful means of invoking Our Lady. Mary herself has called for its recitation many times, most notably at Fatima in 1917.

St. Louis De Montfort, the great and extraordinary preacher of the Rosary said: "Let me place the Rosary around a sinner's neck and he will not escape me." St. Dominic, great promoter of the Rosary said: "A day will come when our Lady will save the world by the Rosary."

THE FIFTEEN PROMISES OF
MARY MOST HOLY TO THOSE
WHO PRAY THE ROSARY

1. Whoever shall faithfully serve me by the recitation of the Rosary shall receive signal graces.

2. I promise my special protection and the greatest graces to all those who shall recite the Rosary.

3. The Rosary shall be a powerful armor against hell; it will destroy vice, decrease sin and defeat heresy.

4. It will cause virtue and good works to flourish; it will obtain for souls the abundant mercy of God; it will withdraw the hearts of men from the love of the world and its vanities, and will lift them to the desire of eternal things. Oh, that souls would sanctify themselves by this means!

5. The soul that recommends itself to me by recitation of the Rosary shall not perish.

6. Whoever shall recite the Rosary devoutly, applying himself to the consideration of its sacred mysteries shall never be conquered by misfortune: if he be a sinner, he shall not perish by an unprovided death; if he be just, he shall remain in the grace of God. He shall become worthy of eternal life.

7. Whoever shall have a true devotion for the Rosary shall not die without the sacraments of the Church.

8. Those who are faithful to the recitation of the Rosary shall have during their life and at their death the light of God and the plenitude of His graces. At the moment of death they shall participate in the merits of the saints in paradise.

9. I shall deliver from purgatory those who have been devoted to the Rosary.

10. The faithful children of the Rosary shall merit a high degree of glory in heaven.

11. You shall obtain all you ask of me by the recitation of the Rosary.

12. All those who propagate the Holy Rosary shall be aided by me in their necessities.

13. I have obtained from my Divine Son that all the advocates of the Rosary shall have for intercessors the entire celestial court during their life and at the hour of death.

14. All who recite the Rosary are my sons, and brothers of my son, Jesus Christ.

15. Devotion to my Rosary is a great sign of predestination.

THE FIVE FIRST SATURDAYS

"Look, my daughter, my Heart is all pierced with thorns, which men drive into it every moment by their blasphemies and ingratitude. Do you at least seek to console me, and let men know that I promise to assist at the hour of death, with the graces necessary for salvation, all those who on the first Saturday of five consecutive months will:

1. *go to confession and receive Holy Communion.*
2. *recite the rosary.*
3. *and keep me company during a quarter of an hour, meditating on the fifteen mysteries of the rosary, with the purpose of making reparation."**

The sacrament of penance must be received within an eight-day period before or after Communion. The fifteen-minute meditation may be on all or on one special mystery. The rosary and meditation may be combined by thinking on each mystery a few minutes before or after reciting the decade. A sermon for the occasion may be substituted for the meditation.

*Words of Our Lady to Sr. Lucia.

FATIMA PRAYERS

PARDON PRAYER
My God, I believe, I adore, I trust and I love Thee! I beg pardon for those who do not believe, do not adore, do not trust and do not love Thee.

EUCHARISTIC PRAYER
Most Holy Trinity, I adore Thee! My God, My God, I love Thee in the Most Blessed Sacrament!

ROSARY DECADE PRAYER
Oh my Jesus, forgive us our sins; save us from the fires of hell; lead all souls to heaven, especially those most in need of Thy mercy.

SACRIFICE PRAYER
Oh my Jesus, it is for love of Thee, in reparation for the offenses committed against the Immaculate Heart of Mary, and for the conversion of poor sinners.

ANGEL'S PRAYER
With the Blessed Sacrament suspended in the air, the angel at Fatima prostrated himself, and recited this prayer:

O Most Holy Trinity, Father, Son and Holy Spirit, I adore Thee profoundly. I offer Thee the most precious Body, Blood, Soul and Divinity of Jesus Christ, present in all the tabernacles of the world, in reparation for the outrages, sacrileges and indifference by which He is offended. By the infinite merits of the Sacred Heart of Jesus and the Immaculate Heart of Mary, I beg the conversion of poor sinners.

OUR LADY OF FATIMA
NOVENA PRAYER

Most Holy Virgin, who deigned to come to Fatima to reveal the treasure of graces hidden in the recitation of the Rosary, inspire my heart with a sincere love of this devotion, that I may obtain the conversion of sinners, the conversion of Russia *(here name the other favors for which you are praying),* which I ask of you in this Novena.

O Mary, I consecrate myself to you and I will wear your Scapular always as a sign of this consecration. I will offer the fulfillment of my daily duties in reparation for sins, particularly those against your Immaculate Heart and against the Eucharistic Heart of Jesus. I desire to be ever more deeply united to His Heart, in the intimacy of your own Immaculate Heart, with each passing moment of my life until the last. Amen.

HOW TO SAY YOUR ROSARY WITH
ST. LOUIS DE MONTFORT

1. *Sign yourself with the Rosary's crucifix, saying at the same time:* "In the Name of the Father, and of the Son, and of the Holy Spirit. Amen."

2. *Recite the following prayer:*

I unite with all the saints in Heaven, with all the just on earth and with all the faithful here present. I unite with Thee, O my Jesus, in order to praise worthily Thy holy Mother and to praise Thee in her and through her. I renounce all the distractions I may have during this rosary which I wish to say with modesty, attention and devotion, just as if it were to be the last of my life.

We offer Thee, O Most Holy Trinity, this Creed in honor of all the mysteries of our Faith; this Our Father and these three Hail Marys in honor of the unity of Thy Essence and the Trinity of Thy Persons. We ask of Thee a lively faith, a firm hope and an ardent charity. Amen.

3. *Recite the Apostles Creed:*

I believe in God, the Father Almighty, Creator of heaven and earth. And in Jesus Christ His only Son, Our Lord, Who was conceived by the Holy Spirit, born of the Virgin Mary, suffered under Pontius Pilate, was crucified, died and was buried. He descended into hell, the third day He arose again from the dead. He ascended into heaven, and sitteth at the right hand of God, the Father Almighty, from whence He shall come to judge the living and the dead.

I believe in the Holy Spirit, the Holy Catholic Church, the communion of saints, the forgiveness of sins, the resurrection of the body and life everlasting. Amen.

4. *Recite one Our Father and Three Hail Marys:*

Our Father, Who art in heaven, hallowed be Thy name. Thy kingdom come. Thy will be done, on earth as it is in heaven. Give us this day our daily bread, and forgive us our trespasses, as we forgive those who trespass against us. And lead us not into temptation, but deliver us from evil. Amen.

Hail Mary, full of grace, the Lord is with thee. Blessed art thou among women, and blessed is the fruit of thy womb, Jesus. Holy Mary, Mother of God, pray for us sinners, now and at the hour of our death. Amen. *(Three times)*

5. *Recite the Lesser Doxology:*

Glory be to the Father, and to the Son, and to the Holy Spirit. As it was in the beginning, is now and ever shall be, world without end. Amen.

6. *Now begin the actual Rosary, which consists of 15 decades. Five of these decades make one complete Rosary, however. Each decade is composed of the following:*

One Our Father
Ten Hail Marys
One Glory be to the Father

THE LIFE, DEATH AND GLORY OF JESUS AND MARY IN THE MOST HOLY ROSARY

I BELIEVE IN GOD

1. *Faith in the presence of God.*
2. *Faith in the Gospel.*
3. *Faith and obedience to the Pope, as Vicar of Jesus Christ.*

OUR FATHER

God is present everywhere, One, Living and True.

HAIL MARY

1. To honor the Eternal Father, Who, in contemplating Himself, brings forth His Son.
2. To honor the Eternal Word, equal to His Father, Who together with Him, in mutual Love, brings forth the Holy Spirit.
3. To honor the Holy Spirit, Who proceeds from the mutual love of the Father and the Son.

THE FIVE JOYFUL MYSTERIES

✝ ✝ ✝

The Annunciation

THE FIRST JOYFUL MYSTERY
We offer Thee, O Lord Jesus, this first decade in honor of Thy Incarnation in Mary's womb, and we ask of Thee, through this Mystery and through her intercession, a profound humility. Amen.

The Annunciation

Our Father: - *Charity of God.*
Immense.

1. To deplore the unhappy state of the disobedient Adam; his own just condemnation as well as that of all his children.
2. To honor the desires of the patriarchs and prophets who longed for the Messias.
3. To honor the wishes and prayers of the Blessed Virgin for the speedy coming of the Messias and to honor her marriage with Saint Joseph.
4. To honor the charity of the Eternal Father Who gave up His Son.
5. To honor the love of the Son Who delivered Himself up for us.
6. To honor the mission and the salutation of the Angel Gabriel.
7. To honor the virginal fear of Mary.
8. To honor the faith and the consent of Mary.
9. To honor the creation of the soul and the formation of the body of Jesus Christ in the womb of Mary, by the operation of the Holy Spirit.
10. To honor the adoration by the angels of the Word Incarnate in the womb of Mary.

May the grace of the mystery of the Annunciation come down into our souls.
Amen.

The Visitation

THE SECOND JOYFUL MYSTERY
We offer Thee, O Lord Jesus, this second decade in honor of the Visitation of Thy holy Mother to her cousin St. Elizabeth and the sanctification of St. John the Baptist, and we ask of Thee, through this Mystery and through the intercession of Thy holy Mother, charity towards our neighbor. Amen.

The Visitation

Our Father: *- Majesty of God.*
Adorable.

1. To honor the joy of the heart of Mary in the possession of Jesus.
2. To honor the sacrifice that Jesus Christ made of Himself to His Eternal Father by coming into this world.
3. To honor the love Jesus and Mary had for each other.
4. To recall Saint Joseph's doubts concerning Mary's pregnancy.
5. To honor the choice of the Elect, planned by Jesus and Mary.
6. To honor the fervor of Mary in her visit to her cousin, St. Elizabeth.
7. To honor the salutation of Mary and the sanctification of St. John the Baptist and of his mother, St. Elizabeth.
8. To honor the gratitude of the Blessed Virgin toward God in the "Magnificat."
9. To honor her charity and humility in serving her cousin.
10. To honor the mutual dependence of Jesus and Mary and that which we should have in regard to Them.

May the grace of the Mystery of the Visitation come down into our souls. Amen.

The Nativity

THE THIRD JOYFUL MYSTERY

We offer Thee, O Lord Jesus, this third decade in honor of Thy Nativity in the stable of Bethlehem, and we ask of Thee, through this Mystery and through the intercession of Thy Holy Mother, detachment from the things of the world, contempt of riches and love of poverty. Amen.

The Nativity

Our Father: - Riches of God.
Infinite.

1. To honor Mary and Joseph in the contempt and rejection they suffered in Bethlehem.
2. To honor the poverty of the stable in which God was born.
3. To honor the deep contemplation and the immense love of Mary.
4. To honor the virginal birth of Jesus.
5. To honor the adoration and the canticles of the Angels at the birth of Jesus Christ.
6. To honor the enchanting beauty of His divine infancy.
7. To honor the coming of the shepherds, bringing their gifts to the stable.
8. To honor the circumcision of Jesus.
9. To honor the imposition of the name of Jesus and its grandeur.
10. To honor the adoration of the Magi Kings and their presents.

May the grace of the Mystery of the Nativity come down into our souls. Amen.

The Presentation in the Temple

THE FOURTH JOYFUL MYSTERY

We offer Thee, O Lord Jesus, this fourth decade in honor of Thy Presentation in the Temple and the Purification of Mary, and we ask of Thee through this Mystery and through the intercession of Thy Holy Mother, great purity of body and soul. Amen.

The Presentation in the Temple

Our Father: *- Wisdom of God.*
Eternal.

1. To honor the obedience of Jesus and Mary to the law.
2. To honor the sacrifice that Mary made of His humanity.
3. To honor the sacrifice that Mary made of her reputation.
4. To honor the joy and the canticles of Simeon and Anna, the Prophetess.
5. To honor the ransoming of Jesus Christ through the offering of two turtle doves.
6. To recall the massacre of the Holy Innocents by the cruelty of Herod.
7. To honor the flight of Jesus Christ to Egypt, and the obedience of St. Joseph to the voice of the Angel.
8. To honor His mysterious stay in Egypt.
9. To honor His return to Nazareth.
10. To honor His growing in age and wisdom.

May the grace of the Mystery of the Presentation in the Temple come down into our souls. Amen.

The Finding of Our Lord in the Temple

THE FIFTH JOYFUL MYSTERY

We offer Thee, O Lord Jesus, this fifth decade in honor of Mary's finding Thee in the Temple, and we ask of Thee, through this Mystery and through the intercession of Thy Holy Mother, the gift of true wisdom. Amen.

The Finding of Our Lord in the Temple

Our Father: - *Sanctity of God.*
Incomprehensible.

1. To honor Jesus' hidden life, laborious and obedient in His home at Nazareth.
2. To honor His preaching and His being found in the Temple among the doctors.
3. To honor His baptism by St. John the Baptist.
4. To honor His fast and temptation in the desert.
5. To honor His admirable preaching.
6. To honor His astonishing miracles.
7. To honor the choice of His twelve apostles and the powers He gives them.
8. To honor His marvelous transfiguration.
9. To honor His washing the feet of the Apostles.
10. To honor the institution of the Holy Eucharist.

May the grace of the Mystery of the Finding of Our Lord in the Temple come down into our souls. Amen.

The Presentation

THE FIVE LUMINOUS MYSTERIES

The Baptism of Jesus

THE FIRST LUMINOUS MYSTERY

We offer Thee, O Lord Jesus, this decade in honor of our baptismal commitment, and we ask of Thee, through this Mystery and through the intercession of Thy most holy Mother, the grace of faithfulness to our baptismal promises. Amen.

The Baptism of Jesus

Our Father: *- Fidelity to God.*

1. John the Baptist: "I am the voice of one crying out in the desert." (Jn 1:23)
2. "After me comes He who is mightier than I." (Mk 1:7)
3. "I baptize you with water . . . He will baptize you with the Holy Spirit and with fire. (Mt 3:11)
4. John proclaimed, "Behold the Lamb of God who takes away the sins of the world!" (Jn 1:29)
5. Jesus came to John, to be baptized by him. (Mt 3:13)
6. "I need to be baptized by You, and do You come to me?" (Mt 3:14)
7. Jesus came to him. "Allow it for now." (Mt 3:15)
8. After Jesus was baptized, "the Spirit of God descended like a dove upon Him." (Mt 3:16)
9. A voice came from heaven: "This is My beloved Son, with whom I am well pleased." (Mt 3:17)
10. "The Spirit drove Him out into the desert . . . where He remained for forty days." (Mk 1:12-13)

May the grace of fidelity to our baptismal promises come down into our souls. Amen.

The Wedding Feast at Cana

THE SECOND LUMINOUS MYSTERY
We offer Thee, O Lord Jesus, this decade in honor of Your first public miracle at the Wedding Feast at Cana, and we ask of Thee through this Mystery and through Mary's intercession the grace to do whatever You tell us. Amen.

The Wedding Feast at Cana
Our Father: - *Obedience.*

1. "There was a marriage at Cana in Galilee." (Jn 2:1)
2. When the wine failed, the Mother of Jesus said to Him, "They have no wine." (Jn 2:3)
3. And Jesus said to her, "Woman, My hour has not yet come." (Jn 2:4)
4. His Mother then said to the servers, "Do whatever He tells you." (Jn 2:5)
5. "Now there were six stone water jars, each holding twenty to thirty gallons." (Jn 2:6)
6. Jesus told them, "Fill the jars with water." So they filled them to the brim. (Jn 2:7)
7. Then He told them, "Draw some out now and take it to the chief steward." (Jn 2:8)
8. "And when the chief steward tasted the water that had become wine, he called the bridegroom." (Jn 2:9)
9. He said to him, "Everyone serves the good wine first. You have kept the good wine until now." (Jn 2:10)
10. "Jesus did this as the beginning of His signs in Cana of Galilee." (Jn 2:11)

May the grace of obedience to the teachings of the Church come down into our souls. Amen.

The Proclamation of the Kingdom

THE THIRD LUMINOUS MYSTERY
We offer Thee, O Lord Jesus, this decade in honor of Thy proclamation of the Kingdom of God, and we ask Thee, through the Mystery and through the intercession of Thy most holy Mother, the grace to approach the sacrament of Reconciliation with humility. Amen.

The Proclamation of the Kingdom

Our Father: - *Penance and Humility*

1. Jesus came to Galilee proclaiming the gospel of God. (Mk 1:14)
2. "The light shines in the darkness, and the darkness does not comprehend it." (Jn 1:4-5)
3. Jesus said, "The time is fulfilled and the Kingdom of God is at hand." (Mk 1:15)
4. "Many gathered together . . . and He preached the word to them." (Mk 2:2)
5. Unable to get near Jesus, some men opened up the roof above Him. (Mk 2:4)
6. "Which is easier to say to the paralytic, 'Your sins are forgiven,' or to say, 'Rise, pick up your mat and walk?'" (Mk 2:9)
7. He said to the paralytic, "I say to you, rise, pick up your mat and go home." (Mk 2:10-11)
8. Jesus called the twelve and gave them authority over unclean spirits. (Mt 10:1)
9. Jesus told His disciples, "The Kingdom of heaven is at hand." (Mt 10:5)
10. "Whose sins you forgive are forgiven, and whose sins you retain are retained." (Jn 20:22-23)

May the grace of the mystery of the Sacrament of mercy and reconciliation come down into our souls. Amen.

The Transfiguration

THE FOURTH LUMINOUS MYSTERY

We offer Thee, O Lord Jesus, this decade in honor of Thy Transfiguration on Mt. Tabor, and we ask of Thee, through this Mystery and through the intercession of Thy most holy Mother, the grace to listen to Jesus as the Father commanded the apostles to do. Amen.

The Transfiguration

Our Father: - *The Majesty of God.*

1. "Jesus took with Him Peter, John and James, and went up on the mountain to pray." (Lk 9:28)
2. "And Jesus was transfigured before them." (Mt 17:2)
3. "And behold there appeared to them Moses and Elijah talking with Him." (Mt 17:3)
4. "They spoke of Jesus' exodus, that He was going to accomplish in Jerusalem." (Lk 9:31)
5. Then Peter said to Jesus, "Lord, it is good that we are here." (Mt 17:4)
6. "As he said this, a cloud came and overshadowed them." (Lk 9:34)
7. From the cloud came a voice that said, "This is My beloved Son: listen to Him." (Lk 9:35)
8. "Suddenly, looking around, they no longer saw anyone but Jesus, alone with them." (Mk 9:8)
9. "Tell no man, until the Son of Man is risen from the dead." (Mk 9:9)
10. "So they kept the matter to themselves." Mk 9:10)

May the grace of the Transfiguration come down into our souls. Amen.

The Institution of the Holy Eucharist

THE FIFTH LUMINOUS MYSTERY

We offer Thee, O Lord Jesus, this decade in honor of Thine Institution of the Sacrament of the Eucharist, and we ask of Thee, through this Mystery and through the intercession of Thy most Holy Mother, a greater faith in Thy Real Presence in the Eucharist. Amen.

The Institution of the Holy Eucharist

Our Father: *- Devotion to Our Lord*
in the Eucharist

1. The disciples approached Jesus and said, "Where shall we prepare the Passover meal?" (Mt 26:17)
2. Jesus said, "Go into the city to a certain man." (Mt 26:18)
3. He said to them, "I have eagerly desired to eat this Passover with you."(Lk 22:14)
4. At supper He said, "Amen, I say to you, one of you will betray Me." (Mt 26:21)
5. Then Judas, His betrayer, said in reply, "Is it I, Rabbi?" (Mt 26:25)
6. Jesus took bread, broke it, and giving it to His disciples said, "Take and eat; this is My Body."(Mt 26:26)
7. He took the cup saying, "Drink from it, all of you, for this is My Blood." (Mt 26:27)
8. "As often as you eat this bread and drink this cup, you proclaim the death of the Lord until He comes." (1 Cor 11:26)
9. "I am the Living Bread that came down from heaven. Whoever eats this bread will live forever." (Jn 6:51)
10. "Whoever eats My Flesh and drinks My Blood has eternal life, and I will raise him up on the last day." (Jn 6:54)

May the grace of the Mystery of Christ's presence in the Eucharist come down into our souls. Amen.   114k

Our Lady Crowned by an Angel (A. Dürer)

THE FIVE SORROWFUL MYSTERIES

✝ ✝ ✝

The Agony in the Garden

THE FIRST SORROWFUL MYSTERY

We offer Thee, O Lord Jesus, this sixth decade in honor of Thy Agony in the Garden of Olives, and we ask of Thee, through this Mystery and through the intercession of Thy Holy Mother, contrition for our sins. Amen.

116

Our Father: - *Happiness of God. Essential.*

1. To honor the divine retreats made by our Lord during His life, especially in the garden of agony.
2. To honor the humble, fervent prayers offered by our Lord during His life and on the eve of His passion.
3. To honor the patience and kindness with which He treated His Apostles especially in the Garden of Olives.
4. To honor the loneliness of His soul during His whole life especially in the Garden.
5. To honor the streams of blood into which anguish plunged Him.
6. To honor the consolation He greatly desired from an angel.
7. To honor His conformity to the will of His Father, despite the repugnance of nature.
8. To honor the courage with which He approaches His executioners, and the force of speech by which He threw them down and then raised them up again.
9. His betrayal by Judas and His captivity by the Jews.
10. His abandonment by His Apostles.

   May the grace of the Mystery of the Agony in the Garden come down into our souls. Amen.

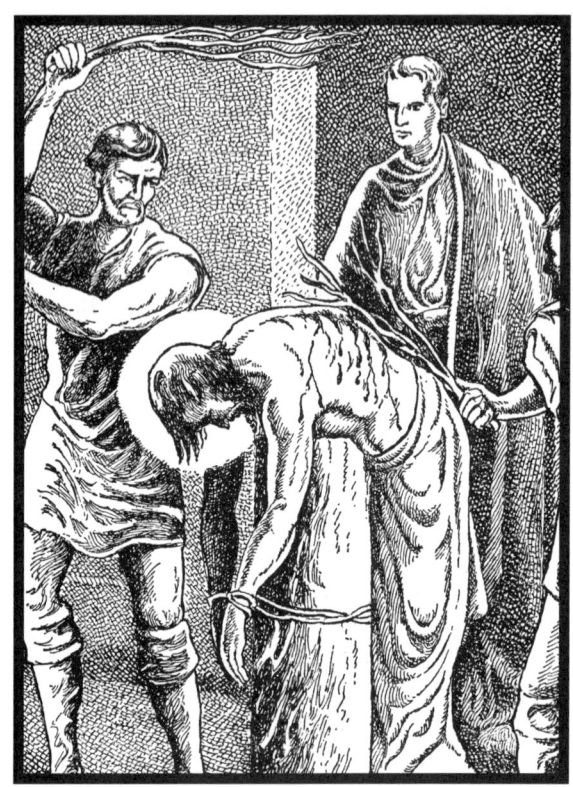

The Scourging

THE SECOND SORROWFUL MYSTERY
We offer Thee, O Lord Jesus, this seventh decade in honor of Thy bloody Scourging and we ask of Thee, through this Mystery and through the intercession of Thy Holy Mother, the grace of mortifying our senses. Amen.

Our Father: - *Patience of God.*
Admirable.

1. To honor Christ as He is bound with the chains and cords.
2. To honor Christ as He is slapped in the face.
3. To honor Christ in the denials of St. Peter.
4. To honor Christ in the ignominies which He received at Herod's court, when He was clothed with a white robe.
5. To honor Christ in the stripping of His clothes.
6. To honor Christ for the contempt and insults He received from the executioners.
7. To honor Christ beaten and torn by the knotty rods and the cruel whips.
8. To honor the column to which He was tied.
9. To honor the blood which He shed and the wounds He received.
10. To honor His collapse in His own blood.

May the grace of the Mystery of the Scourging come down into our souls. Amen.

The Crowning with Thorns

THE THIRD SORROWFUL MYSTERY
We offer Thee, O Lord Jesus, this eighth decade in honor of Thy being crowned with thorns, and we ask of Thee, through this Mystery and through the intercession of Thy Holy Mother, contempt of the world. Amen.

120

The Crowning with Thorns

Our Father: - *Beauty of God.*
Unspeakable.

1. To honor Christ being stripped for the third time.
2. To honor His crown of thorns.
3. To honor the veil with which they bound His eyes.
4. To honor Christ for the blows and spittle with which they covered His face.
5. To honor the old cloak which they placed upon His shoulders.
6. To honor the reed which they placed in His hands.
7. To honor the column stump upon which He was tied.
8. To honor Christ for the outrages and insults offered Him.
9. To honor Christ for the blows which He received upon His adorable head.
10. To honor Christ for the derision of which He was the object.

May the grace of the Mystery of the Crowning with Thorns come down into our souls. Amen.

The Carrying of the Cross

THE FOURTH SORROWFUL MYSTERY

We offer Thee, O Lord Jesus, this ninth decade in honor of Thy carrying the Cross, and we ask of Thee, through this Mystery and through the intercession of Thy Holy Mother, patience in bearing our crosses. Amen.

The Carrying of the Cross

Our Father: - *The Omnipotence of God. Boundless.*

1. To honor our Lord's presentation before the populace, the "Ecce Homo."
2. To honor Our Lord for the insult of the preference of Barabbas to His Person.
3. To honor Our Lord as the false witnesses testify against Him.
4. To honor Our Lord in His condemnation to death.
5. To honor the love with which He embraced and kissed His Cross.
6. To honor the tremendous pains He suffered in carrying it.
7. To honor His falls, due to weakness, beneath His burden.
8. To honor the sorrowful meeting with His Holy Mother.
9. To honor the veil of Veronica, upon which His features were imprinted.
10. To honor His tears, those of His Holy Mother, and of the holy women who followed Him to Calvary.

May the grace of the Mystery of the Carrying of the Cross come down into our souls. Amen.

The Crucifixion

THE FIFTH SORROWFUL MYSTERY

We offer Thee, O Lord Jesus, this tenth decade in honor of Thy Crucifixion and ignominious death on Calvary, and we ask of Thee, through this Mystery and through the intercession of Thy Holy Mother, the conversion of sinners, the perseverance of the just, and the relief of the souls in Purgatory. Amen.

The Crucifixion

Our Father: - *Justice of God.*
Tremendous.

1. To honor the five wounds of Our Lord and His blood shed upon the Cross.
2. To honor His pierced Heart and the Cross upon which He was crucified.
3. To honor the nails and the spear that pierced Him, the sponge and the gall and also the vinegar which He was given to drink.
4. To honor Christ for the shame and infamy which He suffered in being crucified between two thieves.
5. To honor the compassion of His Holy Mother.
6. To honor His seven last words.
7. To honor His abandonment and silence.
8. To honor the distress of the whole universe.
9. To honor His cruel and ignominious death.
10. To honor His descent from the Cross and His burial.

May the grace of the Mystery of the Crucifixion come down into our souls. Amen.

The Passion (Albrecht Dürer)

THE FIVE GLORIOUS MYSTERIES

The Resurrection

THE FIRST GLORIOUS MYSTERY

We offer Thee, O Lord Jesus, this eleventh decade in honor of Thy glorious Resurrection and we ask of Thee, through this Mystery and through the intercession of Thy Holy Mother, love of God and fervor in Thy service. Amen.

The Resurrection

Our Father: - *Eternity of God.*
Without beginning.

1. To honor the descent of Our Lord's soul into Limbo.
2. To honor the joy and the release of the souls of the ancient fathers who were in Limbo.
3. To honor the reunion of His soul to His body in His sepulchre.
4. To honor His miraculous departure from His sepulchre.
5. To honor His victory over death and sin, the world and the devil.
6. To honor the four glorious qualities of His body.
7. To honor the power which He received from His Father in heaven and on earth.
8. To honor the apparitions with which He honored His holy Mother, His apostles and His disciples.
9. To honor the communications He had with heaven and the meal He had with His disciples.
10. To honor the authority and the mission which He gave them to go and preach throughout the whole world.

May the grace of the Mystery of the Resurrection come down into our souls. Amen.

The Ascension

THE SECOND GLORIOUS MYSTERY
We offer Thee, O Lord Jesus, this twelfth decade in honor of Thy triumphant Ascension, and we ask of Thee, through this Mystery and through the intercession of Thy Holy Mother, an ardent desire for Heaven, our true home. Amen.

The Ascension

Our Father: - *The Immensity of God.*
Limitless.

1. To honor the promise that Christ would send the Holy Spirit.
2. To honor the reunion of all His disciples upon the Mount of Olives.
3. To honor the blessing which He gave them as he ascended into heaven.
4. To honor His glorious Ascension into heaven, by His own proper power.
5. To honor the divine welcome and triumph which He received from God His Father and from the entire celestial court.
6. To honor the triumphant powers with which He opened the gates of heaven.
7. To honor His sitting at the right hand of His Father, equal to Him.
8. To honor the power which He received to judge the living and the dead.
9. To honor His last coming upon earth when His power and Majesty will shine forth in all splendor.
10. To honor the justice which He will exercise at the last judgement, recompensing the good and punishing the wicked for all eternity.

May the grace of the Mystery of the Ascension come down into our souls. Amen.

The Descent of the Holy Spirit

THE THIRD GLORIOUS MYSTERY

We offer Thee, O Lord Jesus, this thirteenth decade in honor of the Mystery of Pentecost, and we ask of Thee, through this Mystery and through the intercession of Thy Holy Mother, the coming of the Holy Spirit into our souls. Amen.

The Descent of the Holy Spirit

Our Father: - *Providence of God.*
Universal.

1. To honor the truth of the Holy Spirit, God, Who proceeds from the Father and the Son.
2. To honor the sending of the Holy Spirit to the apostles.
3. To honor the great noise, with which He descended, a sign of His force and power.
4. To honor the tongues of fire sent upon His apostles to give them the knowledge of Scripture and the love of God and their neighbor.
5. To honor the plenitude of graces with which He privileged Mary, His faithful Spouse.
6. To honor His marvelous conduct toward all the saints, and toward the very person of Jesus Christ, Whom He conducted during His whole life.
7. To honor the twelve fruits of the Holy Spirit.
8. To honor the seven gifts of the Holy Spirit.
9. To ask for the gift of wisdom and the coming of His reign in the hearts of men.
10. To obtain victory over the three evil spirits: the world, the flesh and the devil.

May the grace of the mystery of Pentecost come down into our souls. Amen.

The Assumption

THE FOURTH GLORIOUS MYSTERY

We offer Thee, O Lord Jesus, this fourteenth decade in honor of the resurrection and triumphant Assumption of Thy Holy Mother into heaven and we ask of Thee, through this Mystery and through her intercession, a tender devotion for so good a Mother. Amen.

The Assumption

Our Father: - *Liberality of God.*
Unspeakable.

1. To honor the eternal predestination of Mary as the masterpiece of God's hands.
2. To honor her Immaculate Conception and the fullness of grace and reason in the womb of her mother, St. Anne.
3. To honor her nativity which has gladdened the world.
4. To honor her presentation and her stay in the Temple.
5. To honor her admirable life, exempt from all sin.
6. To honor the plenitude of her singular virtues.
7. To honor her fruitful virginity and painless childbirth.
8. To honor her divine Maternity and her alliance with the Holy Trinity.
9. To honor her precious and loving death.
10. To honor her Resurrection and triumphant Assumption.

May the grace of the Mystery of the Assumption come down into our souls. Amen.

The Coronation of the Blessed Virgin

THE FIFTH GLORIOUS MYSTERY

We offer Thee, O Lord Jesus, this fifteenth decade in honor of the Coronation of Thy Holy Mother, and we ask of Thee, through this Mystery and through her intercession, perseverance in grace and a crown of glory hereafter. Amen.

The Coronation of the Blessed Virgin

Our Father: - Glory to God.
Inaccessible.

1. To honor the triple crown with which the Holy Trinity crowned Mary.
2. To honor the new joy and glory that heaven received by her triumph.
3. To confess her the Queen of heaven and earth, of angels and of men.
4. To honor her as the treasurer and dispenser of God's graces, of the merits of Jesus Christ and of the gifts of the Holy Spirit.
5. To honor her as the mediatrix and advocate of men.
6. To honor her as the destroyer and ruin of the devil and of heresies.
7. To honor her as the sure refuge of sinners.
8. To honor her as the Mother and support of Christians.
9. To honor her as the joy and sweetness of the just.
10. To honor her as the universal refuge of the living, the all powerful comfort of the afflicted, the dying and the souls in Purgatory.

May the grace of the Mystery of the Coronation of the Blessed Virgin come down into our souls. Amen.

CONCLUDING PRAYERS

Hail, Holy Queen

Hail Holy Queen, Mother of Mercy, our life, our sweetness and our hope. To thee do we cry, poor banished children of Eve. To thee do we send up our sighs, mourning and weeping in this valley of tears. Turn then, most gracious advocate, thine eyes of mercy towards us. And after this our exile, show unto us the blessed fruit of thy womb, Jesus. O clement, O loving, O sweet Virgin Mary.

Let Us Pray

O God, Who, by the life, death and resurrection of Thy only-begotten Son, has purchased for us the rewards of eternal salvation, grant we beseech Thee, that meditating on these mysteries of the most holy Rosary, we may imitate what they contain and obtain what they promise, through the same Christ our Lord. Amen.

Prayer which may be recited
after the Rosary

Hail Mary, beloved Daughter of the Eternal Father, admirable Mother of the Son, faithful Spouse of the Holy Spirit, august Temple of the Most Holy Trinity! Hail, sovereign Princess, to whom all owe subjection in heaven and on earth! Hail, sure Refuge of Sinners, Our Lady of Mercy, who has never refused any request. All sinful though I am, I cast myself at thy feet and beseech thee to obtain from Jesus, thy beloved Son, contrition and pardon for all my sins, as well as the gift of divine wisdom. I consecrate myself entirely to thee with all that I have. I choose thee today for my Mother and Mistress. Treat me, then, as the least of thy children and the most obedient of thy servants. Listen, my Princess, listen to the sighs of a heart that desires to love and serve thee faithfully. Let it never be said that of all those who have had recourse to thee, I was the first to be abandoned. O my hope, O my life, O my faithful and Immaculate Virgin Mary, defend me, nourish me, hear me, teach me and save me. Amen.

LITANY OF THE BLESSED VIRGIN MARY

Lord, have mercy on us.
   Christ, have mercy on us.
Lord, have mercy on us.
Christ, hear us.
   Christ, graciously hear us.
God the Father of Heaven,
   Have mercy on us.
God the Son, Redeemer of the world,
   Have mercy on us.
God the Holy Spirit,
   Have mercy on us.
Holy Trinity, one God,
   Have mercy on us.
Holy Mary, pray for us.
Holy Mother of God, pray for us.
Holy Virgin of virgins, etc.
Mother of Christ, Mother of the Church,
Mother of divine grace, Mother most pure,
Mother most chaste, Mother inviolate,
Mother undefiled, Mother most amiable,
Mother most admirable,
Mother of good counsel,
Mother of our Creator,
Mother of our Savior,
Virgin most prudent,
Virgin most venerable,
Virgin most renowned,
Virgin most powerful,
Virgin most merciful, Virgin most faithful,
Mirror of justice, Seat of wisdom,

Cause of our joy, Spiritual vessel,
Vessel of honor,
Singular vessel of devotion, Mystical rose,
Tower of David, Tower of ivory,
House of gold, Ark of the Covenant,
Gate of Heaven, Morning star,
Health of the sick, pray for us.
Refuge of sinners, etc.
Comforter of the afflicted,
Help of Christians,
Queen of angels, Queen of patriarchs,
Queen of prophets, Queen of apostles,
Queen of martyrs, Queen of confessors,
Queen of virgins, Queen of all saints,
Queen conceived without Original Sin,
Queen assumed into Heaven,
Queen of the most holy Rosary,
Queen of peace,

Lamb of God, who takest away the sins of
the world,
    Spare us, O Lord.
Lamb of God, who takest away the sins of
the world,
    Graciously hear us, O Lord.
Lamb of God, who takest away the sins of
the world,
    Have mercy on us.
Pray for us, O Holy Mother of God.
    That we may be made worthy of the
    promises of Christ.

Let us pray.

Grant, we beseech Thee, O Lord God, that we Thy servants may enjoy perpetual health of mind and body, and by the glorious intercession of the Blessed Mary, ever Virgin, be delivered from present sorrow and enjoy eternal happiness. Through Christ Our Lord. Amen.

THE PRO-LIFE ROSARY

The Pro-Life Rosary has the same number of beads as an ordinary rosary, but the colors of the beads have a special symbolism as described below. By using this rosary you maintain the witness that it provides because all who see it know what you are praying for and where you stand on preserving the lives of unborn children.

On the Crucifix say:

Lord, for all those who say "I don't believe, I say "I believe in God. . ."

Then continue with the Apostles' Creed.

Offer the first Our Father, on the white or clear bead, for the intentions of Our Holy Father, the Pope.

The next three beads are purple to symbolize Our Lord's Passion and Death. Say the following prayer before the three Hail Marys.

Lord, I offer these three Hail Marys for an increase in Faith, Hope and Love in all people so that they will always CHOOSE LIFE, and I also offer them in reparation for the suffering You endure each time an unborn baby is killed, each time someone is euthanized, each time death overcomes life in this world. Amen.

143

The Pro-Life Rosary

The First Decade *(alternating aqua-blue and white or clear beads). State the Mysteries of the day: Monday and Thursday, the Joyful Mysteries; Tuesday and Friday, the Sorrowful Mysteries; Wednesday, Saturday and Sunday, the Glorious Mysteries.*

State the Mystery of the day and then say the following prayer:

Dear Lord, dear Mother Mary, every aqua bead is special, for on it I pray a Hail Mary for the intentions of the Immaculate Heart of Mary, and on every white (or clear) bead I say a Hail Mary for peace in our world. Most Sacred Heart of Jesus, have mercy on us! Mary, Queen of Peace, pray for us. Amen.

One Our Father and ten Hail Marys.

The Second Decade *(alternating red and white or clear beads).*

State the Mystery of the day and then say the following prayer:

Jesus, Source of Mercy, Mary, Bearer of Mercy, on every red Hail Mary I pray in reparation for the blood spilled from every baby wrenched from its mother's womb through abortion. I know that even as You hold and comfort each of these precious little ones, the horror of their slaughter screams for justice to be meted out upon our world. May these red Hail Marys be a source of reparation for our sin. I also offer each white (or clear) Hail Mary for the mothers and fathers of these aborted little ones, that they may receive the grace to repent of this sin, turn to Jesus, and receive the gift of salvation with open hearts. Heal them of the emotional and psychological wounds that this sin has caused as You pour out the graces of conversion upon them. Let them now witness for life! Amen.

One Our Father and ten Hail Marys.

The Third Decade *(alternating black and white or clear beads). The black beads are symbolic of the entire medical profession that participates in pro-death activities: all doctors, nurses and assistants; helpers of every type that contribute to abortion, euthanasia and anti-life practices of every sort. Every white (or clear) Hail Mary is for their conversion, repentance and courage in standing against this crimson tide of death!*

State the Mystery of the day and then say the following prayer:

Lord Jesus, Mother Mary, in this decade I offer reparation for all the sins of the medical personnel who act in the interests of death in our society and in our world. I plead also for their conversion to Your truth. Let them see the reality of what they are doing, see the horror of it, rend their hearts in repentance, then work for Life and for You, Jesus, all the rest of their days. Amen.

One Our Father and ten Hail Marys.

The Fourth Decade *(alternating red, white or clear, and blue beads.*

State the Mystery of the day and then say the following prayer:

Lord Jesus, Source of all Truth, Mary, Our Lady of all peoples, with every red Hail Mary I pray that every bad, anti-life law in our nation and world be reversed. With every white (or clear) Hail Mary I plead protection and strengthening of every pro-life law in existence, and with every blue Hail Mary I petition for new and strong pro-life laws to be enacted in our nation and in our world. Amen.

One Our Father and ten Hail Marys.

The Fifth Decade (alternating green and white or clear beads). The color green is symbolic of hope. Our Hope is Jesus Christ and the Life in the Holy Spirit which He offers to us if we but receive it. Because of our hope in Jesus, we have faith that one day our hope for mercy, justice, truth, peace and life will be fully realized.

State the Mystery of the day and then say the following prayer:

Lord Jesus, I thank You for Your Incarnation in our human flesh. You were formed in the womb of the Blessed Virgin Mary. Your humanity at the moment of Your conception gives us, each and every one, humanity at the moment of our conception. Had Satan had his way, You too would have been torn from Your mother's womb, never to be born, and never to fulfill Your destiny in the particular manner in which You did fulfill it. On every green Hail Mary I thank You for those who in any way work for life. Give them continued courage, strength, peace of heart and love. Protect them from all evil and increase their witness in this nation and in this world. Strengthen their families to understand the importance of their work and to support them in their stand for life.

Mother Mary, our mother, under the titles of Our Lady of Guadalupe, Mother of Perpetual Help and Queen of Peace join us in our intercession for the end of all pro-death, pro-choice activities. Crush the head of evil in our nation, our world and in our personal lives. Roll back the crimson holocaust. With every white (or clear) Hail Mary of this decade advance the cause of your Divine Son, Jesus, the Incarnate Word! Stay the hand of chastisement, and if it must fall, protect your children! Amen.

One Our Father and ten Hail Marys.

WORLD MISSION ROSARY

The purpose of the World Mission Rosary is to pray for world peace and conversion. The five decades are in five colors to represent the five continents for which we pray.

> *The green decade is for Africa.*
> *The red decade is for the Americas.*
> *The white decade is for Europe.*
> *The blue decade is for Oceania.*
> *The yellow decade is for Asia.*

Say three final Hail Marys for the missioners throughout the world, the true instruments of the union of all people in the name of and with the grace of Jesus.

Your prayer should not be selfish. Pray for everyone: for those who resist God and for those who do not know Him; for the indifferent Christian and for those who languish in prison; for those who have neither home, nor food, nor work. Pray that all may receive honesty of life, faith, peace and well being.

God will grant your prayer if you ask for these graces through the intercession of Mary.

The Blessed Mother said at Fatima: "Pray the rosary every day. Pray for the world and for peace. Only my Immaculate Heart can help you."

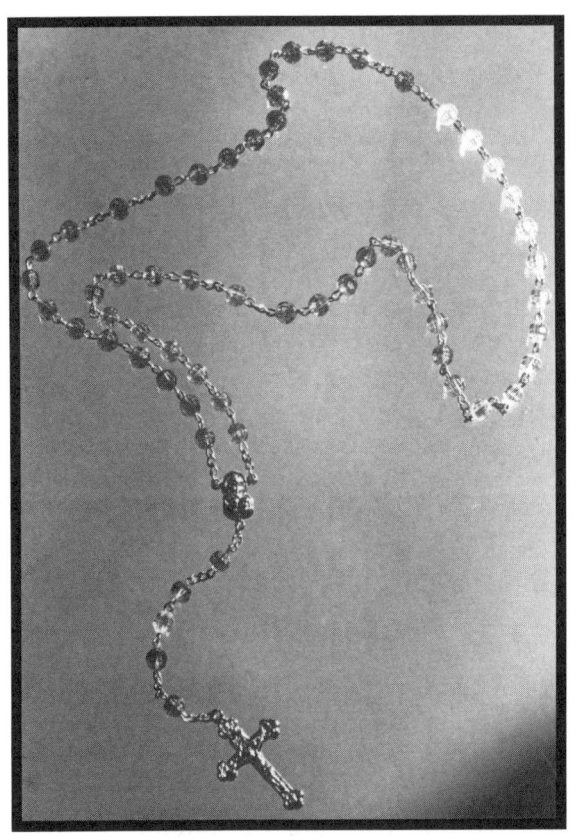

World Mission Rosary

(If you would like to purchase a World Mission Rosary or would like further information, you may contact: Fatima Shrine, P. O. Box 5857, 101 Summer Street, Holliston, MA 01746. Tel. (508) 429-2144. Gift Shop: (508) 429-8172.)

A CHILD'S ROSARY

This rosary was composed by Rev. Malachy Augustin Toner, S.S.C. of Our Lady of Apostles Convent, Rostrevor, County Down, Ireland. It was approved by Archbishop Sean Brady of Armagh on April 3, 1998.

Meditation on the Mysteries has always been the important part of the Holy Rosary. Whence we meditate briefly on all the Mysteries.

We put the Hail Mary into the mouth of a person involved in the Mystery, and we add the Holy Mary as our part and our petition.

Begin with the Our Father.

The Annunciation

The angel Gabriel enters the little home of Mary in Nazareth, speaks to her softly and says: Hail Mary, full of grace, the Lord is with you. Blessed are you among women, and blessed is the fruit of your womb, Jesus.

And we say: Holy Mary, Mother of God, pray for us sinners now and at the hour of our death. Amen.

The Visitation

Elizabeth hears the voice of Mary who has come to visit her. She rushes out, embraces her and says: Hail Mary, *etc.*

And we say: Holy Mary, *etc.*

The Nativity

The shepherds enter the cave at Bethlehem. They kneel before the crib and adore the Child Jesus. Then they turn to Mary, bless her, and say: Hail Mary, *etc.*

And we say: Holy Mary, *etc.*

The Presentation

Simeon offers the Child Jesus in the Temple. He hands Him gently back to His Mother Mary, blesses her and says: Hail Mary, *etc.*

And we say: Holy Mary, *etc.*

The Finding in the Temple

The teachers and doctors of the law return the lost boy Jesus to Joseph and Mary. As the three depart for home, they bless Mary and say: Hail Mary, *etc.*

And we say: Holy Mary, *etc.*

The Baptism in the Jordan

But John said, "I ought to be baptized by You. Remember, in my mother's womb I leaped for joy at the very sound of Your Mother's voice." Hail Mary, *etc.*

And we say: Holy Mary, *etc.*

The Wedding Feast at Cana

Mary, watchful Mother, whispered to Jesus, "They have no wine." Later, the steward exclaimed, "You have kept the best to the last." After the feast, alone with Mary, the young couple gave thanks and said: Hail Mary, *etc.*

And we say: Holy Mary, *etc.*

The Preaching of the Kingdom

"Repent and believe," Jesus cried out. "Blessed the womb that bore You," the old woman called back. And the crowd joined in and prayed: Hail Mary, *etc.*

And we say: Holy Mary, *etc.*

The Transfiguration

His face shone like the sun. His clothes gleamed white as snow. His Father's voice: "This is My Beloved Son." Peter, inspired, cried out, "The Child of the Virgin Mother of Nazareth, verily the Son of the Living God." Hail Mary, *etc.*

And we say: Holy Mary, *etc.*

The Institution of the Eucharist

"This is My Body, to be given up for you. Take and eat. This is the Cup of My Blood, to be shed for you. Take and drink. Do this in memory of Me." The apostles exclaim, "The Body and Blood, derived solely from Mary, becomes the source of our Redemption, the Sacrifice of our faith, and the spiritual food of our souls." Hail Mary, *etc.*

And we say: Holy Mary, *etc.*

(Also approved by Archbishop Brady, 8th September, 2003.)

The Agony in the Garden

As the holy women hear of the terrible agony of Jesus and His sweating of blood in the Garden of Gethsemane, they gather around Mary, comfort her and say: Hail Mary, *etc. And we say:* Holy Mary, *etc.*

The Scourging at the Pillar

The Apostle John returns to the little group in the Upper Room and tells them that he has seen Jesus brutally scourged at the pillar. He comforts Mary and says: Hail Mary, *etc. And we say:* Holy Mary, *etc.*

The Crowning with Thorns

Mary Magdalene also comes back and says that she has seen Jesus crowned with thorns and mocked as a king. She comforts Mary and says: Hail Mary *etc.*
And we say: Holy Mary, *etc.*

The Carrying of the Cross

Veronica shows Mary the towel on which is imprinted the suffering face of Christ as He carries His Cross to Calvary. She consoles Mary and says: Hail Mary, etc.
And we say: Holy Mary, *etc.*

The Crucifixion

As Jesus bows His head in death, the good thief blesses Mary from his cross and says: Hail Mary, *etc.*
And we say: Holy Mary, *etc.*

The Resurrection

Jesus appeared early on Easter Sunday morning to His own Mother Mary, smiled upon her, blessed her and said: Hail Mary, *etc. And we say:* Holy Mary, *etc.*

The Ascension

As Jesus ascends into heaven and disappears beyond the clouds, the Apostles gather around Mary. They comfort Her, console themselves and say: Hail Mary, *etc.*
And we say: Holy Mary, *etc.*

The Descent of the Holy Spirit

The Holy Spirit descends upon the Apostles and upon the head of Mary as a flame of fire. He speaks to the heart of Mary and says: Hail Mary, *etc.*
And we say: Holy Mary, *etc.*

The Assumption

The angels carry the body of Mary to heaven, and as they go on their way they sing, and they say, and they pray: Hail Mary, *etc. And we say:* Holy Mary, *etc.*

The Coronation of Mary as Queen of Heaven

As Mary is crowned Queen of Heaven, Queen of Earth, Queen of Angels and Queen of Men, the Father has no better words to speak to Her than the words of the Angel Gabriel, and He says: Hail Mary, *etc. And we say:* Holy Mary, *etc.*

Glory be to the Father, and to the Son, and to the Holy Spirit, as it was in the beginning, is now, and ever shall be, world without end. Amen.

The Brigittine Rosary consists of 6 decades of 10 beads each. There are 3 additional beads at the end. Each decade consists of 1 *Our Father* and 10 *Hail Marys*. The *Apostles' Creed* is said on the Crucifix.

The 63 *Hail Marys* are in remembrance of the 63 years of Mary's earthly life according to one traditional account. The 7 *Our Fathers,* said on the large beads between each decade, are in remembrance of the Seven Sorrows and Seven Joys of the Blessed Virgin.

Our Lady Queen of Heaven

CHAPLETS OF OUR LADY

The Little Crown of the Blessed Virgin Mary

THE LITTLE CROWN
OF THE BLESSED VIRGIN
By St. Louis Mary De Montfort

Preface

St. John, the beloved disciple of Jesus and Mary, was privileged to behold a wonderful sign in heaven: "A woman clothed with the sun, and the moon was under her feet, and upon her head a crown of twelve stars." (Apoc. 12).

Scripture commentators tell us this vision portrays the Blessed Virgin with her virtues and privileges, especially her divine motherhood. This gave rise to the Triple Crown of Twelve Stars of the Blessed Virgin which heaven has blessed with countless favors. St. John Berchmans and many other devoted children of Mary made the Little Crown their daily favorite.

St. Louis Mary de Montfort, universally known for his True Devotion to Mary, embellished the Little Crown by adding to each Hail Mary a distinctive invocation in praise of the Blessed Virgin's excellence, power and goodness, ending with the joyful strain, "Rejoice, O Virgin Mary! Rejoice a thousand times!"

St. De Montfort gave the Little Crown as a morning prayer to both his religious families, the Montfort Fathers and the Daughters of Wisdom. He heartily recommends it to all who embrace the holy and loving slavery to Jesus through Mary. Thus the world over, from the lips of Mary's *favorite children the Little Crown rises like fragrant incense to our Blessed Mother's throne in heaven and returns to earth in showers of divine benediction.*

Since the Blessed Virgin is the spouse of the Holy Spirit, St. De Montfort prefaces the Little Crown with a liturgical invocation to the Holy Spirit.

Introductory Prayer

Come, Holy Spirit, fill the hearts of Thy faithful and kindle within them the fire of Thy love!

V. Send forth Thy Spirit and they shall be created.

R. And Thou shalt renew the face of the earth.

Let us pray.

O God, Who by the light of the Holy Spirit dost instruct the hearts of the faithful, grant us by this same Spirit to relish what is right and ever to rejoice in His consolation, through Christ our Lord. Amen.

I. Crown of Excellence

To honor the divine maternity of the Blessed Virgin, her ineffable virginity, her purity without stain and her innumerable virtues.

V. Grant that I may praise thee, Holy Virgin!

R. Give me strength against thy enemies!

1. Our Father.
   Hail Mary.
   Blessed art thou, O Virgin Mary, who didst hear the Lord, the Creator of the world; thou didst give birth to Him Who made thee and remainest a Virgin forever.
   Rejoice, O Virgin Mary!
   Rejoice a thousand times!
2. Hail Mary.
   O holy and immaculate Virgin, I know not with what praise to extol thee, since thou didst bear in thy womb the very one Whom the heavens cannot contain.
   Rejoice, O Virgin Mary!
   Rejoice a thousand times!
3. Hail Mary.
   Thou art all fair, O Virgin Mary, and there is no stain in thee.
   Rejoice, O Virgin Mary!
   Rejoice a thousand times!
4. Hail Mary.
   Thy virtues, O Virgin, surpass the stars of heaven in number.
   Rejoice, O Virgin Mary!
   Rejoice a thousand times!

Glory be to the Father...

II. Crown of Power

To honor the royalty of the Blessed Virgin, her magnificence, her universal mediation and the strength of her rule.

5. Our Father.
   Hail Mary
   Glory be to thee, O Empress of the world!
   Bring us with thee to the joys of Heaven.
   Rejoice, O Virgin Mary!
   Rejoice a thousand times!
6. Hail Mary.
   Glory be to thee, O treasure house of the Lord's graces! Grant us a share in thy riches.
   Rejoice, 0 Virgin Mary!
   Rejoice a thousand times!
7. Hail Mary.
   Glory be to thee, O Mediatrix between God and man! Through thee may the Almighty be favorable to us.
   Rejoice, O Virgin Mary!
   Rejoice a thousand times!
8. Hail Mary.
   Glory be to thee who destroyest heresies and crushest demons! Be thou our loving guide.
   Rejoice, O Virgin Mary!
   Rejoice a thousand times!
   Glory be to the Father...

III. Crown of Goodness

To honor the mercy of the Blessed Virgin toward sinners, the poor, the just and the dying.

9. Our Father.
    Hail Mary.
    Glory be to thee, O refuge of sinners!
    Intercede for us with God!
    Rejoice, O Virgin Mary!
    Rejoice a thousand times!
10. Hail Mary.
    Glory be to thee, O Mother of Orphans!
    Render the Almighty favorable to us.
    Rejoice, O Virgin Mary!
    Rejoice a thousand times!
11. Hail Mary.
    Glory be to thee, O joy of the just!
    Lead us with thee to the joys of Heaven.
    Rejoice, O Virgin Mary!
    Rejoice a thousand times!
12. Hail Mary.
    Glory be to thee who art ever ready to assist us in life and in death!
    Lead us with thee to the kingdom of Heaven!
    Rejoice, O Virgin Mary!
    Rejoice a thousand times!
    Glory be to the Father.

Hail Mary, Daughter of God the Father; Hail Mary, Mother of God the Son; Hail Mary, Spouse of the Holy Spirit; Hail Mary, Temple of the Most Holy Trinity; Hail Mary, my mistress, my treasure, my joy, Queen of my heart; my Mother, my life, my sweetness, my dearest hope, yea, my heart and my soul! J am all thine, and all that I have is thine, O Virgin blessed above all things! Let thy soul be in me to magnify the Lord; let thy spirit be in me to rejoice in God. Set thyself, O faithful Virgin, as a seal upon my heart, that in thee and through thee I may be found faithful to God. Receive me, O gracious Virgin, among those whom thou lovest and teachest, whom thou leadest, nourishest and protectest as thy children. Grant that for love of thee I may despise all earthly consolations and ever cling to those of Heaven; until through the Holy Ghost, thy faithful Spouse, and through thee, His faithful Spouse, Jesus Christ thy Son be formed in me for the glory of the Father. Amen.

Our Lady of Mercy

CROWN OF TWELVE STARS OF OUR LADY OF MERCY

An ancient devotion of the Order of Our Lady of Mercy based on the Book of Revelation (12:1): "And a great sign appeared in heaven: a woman clothed with the sun, and the moon under her feet, and on her head a crown of twelve stars."

V. Let us praise and give thanks to the most holy Trinity, who has given us to Mary, a woman clothed with the sun, with the moon under her feet, and on her head a crown of twelve stars.

R. Now and forever, Amen.

V. O most holy Virgin of Mercy!

R. Queen of heaven and earth,you neither abandon nor reject anyone, kindly look upon us with your eyes of mercy. Obtain for us from your Divine Son the forgiveness of our sins, so that we may honor you both, here on earth and later in the heavenly homeland. Amen.

God our loving Father, we praise you for the wonders you have accomplished in Mary, our Mother. Grant that we may be your faithful children.
Our Father; Glory Be.

The first distinction of your crown of glory, O Queen of heaven, is being the Father's highly favored one.
Hail Mary.

The second distinction of your crown of glory, O Queen of heaven, is being the Mother of God the Son.
Hail Mary.

The third distinction of your crown of glory, O Queen of heaven, is being the sanctuary of the Holy Spirit.
Hail Mary.

The fourth distinction of your crown of glory, O Queen of heaven, is being immune from the stain of original sin.
Hail Mary.

O most merciful God the Son, in all our needs grant us the grace to be able to call upon Mary, our Mother of Mercy, with strong hope.
Our Father; Glory Be.

Crown of Twelve Stars of Our Lady of Mercy

The fifth distinction of your crown of glory, O Queen of heaven, is to be the handmaid of the Lord.
Hail Mary.

The sixth distinction of your crown of glory, O Queen of heaven, is being the most eminent and totally unique member of the Church.
Hail Mary.

The seventh distinction of your crown of glory, O Queen of heaven, is being the sublime daughter of Zion.
Hail Mary.

The eighth distinction of your crown of glory, O Queen of heaven, is being the Mother of all Christ's members.
Hail Mary.

O God the Holy Spirit, grant us the grace to be able to respond with childlike love to all the gifts that we have received from Mary.
Our Father; Glory Be.

The ninth distinction of your crown of glory, O Queen of heaven, is being the teacher and model of all virtues.
Hail Mary.

The tenth distinction of your crown of glory,
O Queen of heaven, is being associated with
the Lord at the foot of the Cross.
Hail Mary.

The eleventh distinction of your crown of
glory, O Queen of heaven, is being assumed
body and soul into heavenly glory.
Hail Mary.

The twelfth distinction of your crown of
glory, O Queen of heaven, is that you are
exalted by the Lord as Queen of all creation.
Hail Mary.

V. Let us greet Mary, who has done great
   things for us, and say:

R. Hail, Mother of Mercy,
   Comfort of the afflicted,
   Redemptress of captives.
   You are the glory of Jerusalem,
   You are the joy of Israel,
   You are the honor of our people.

V. O blessed Virgin, the Lord has clothed
   you with holiness.

R. Mother of God, intercede for us.

V. Let us pray.
God, the Father of mercies,
You sent Your Son into the world
as Redeemer of the human race;
grant that we who honor His Mother
as Our Lady of Mercy
may faithfully protect
and seek to spread to all peoples
the true liberty of Your children,
which Christ has merited by
His sacrifice.
We ask this through
our Lord Jesus Christ, Your Son,
who lives and reigns with You and the
Holy Spirit, one God, forever and ever.

R. Amen.

V. For the Church,
for the spread of the Faith,
for peace among all peoples,
and for the freedom of captives.

R. Hail, holy Queen.

Chaplets may be obtained by writing to:
Fathers of Our Lady of Mercy
LeRoy, New York, 14482

ROSARY OF MARY'S IMMACULATE HEART

At the beginning:

We make the Sign of the Cross five times in veneration of our Savior's five Holy Wounds.

We say on the large beads (of an ordinary Rosary):

Sorrowful and Immaculate Heart of Mary, Pray for those who seek refuge in you!

On the small beads:

Holy Mother, save us through your Immaculate Heart's Flame of Love!

At the end (three times):

Glory be to the Father, and to the Son, and to the Holy Spirit; as it was in the beginning, is now, and ever shall be, world without end. Amen.

THE CHAPLET OF THE TEN EVANGELICAL VIRTUES OF THE BLESSED VIRGIN MARY

This prayer, contained in the Rule of the Ten Virtues of the Blessed Virgin Mary, has been passed on by tradition in the Marian Order. It is meant for private recitation on the Rosary.

First we make the Sign of the Cross and recite one Our Father, followed by ten Hail Marys.

After the words, Holy Mary, Mother of God, *mention one virtue in the following order:*

1. most pure,
2. most prudent,
3. most humble,
4. most faithful,
5. most devout,
6. most obedient,
7. most poor,
8. most patient,
9. most merciful,
10. most sorrowful,

pray for us sinners, now and at the hour of our death. Amen.

V. Glory be to the Father and to the Son and to the Holy Spirit,

R. As it was in the beginning, is now and ever shall be, world without end. Amen.

V. In your Conception, O Virgin Mary, you were Immaculate.

R. Pray for us to the Father, whose Son, Jesus, you brought forth into the world.

V. Let us pray.

Father, You prepared the Virgin Mary to be the worthy Mother of Your Son. You let her share beforehand in the salvation Christ would bring by His death and kept her sinless from the first moment of her Conception. Help us by her prayers to live in Your presence without sin. We ask this in the Name of Jesus the Lord.

R. Amen.

V. May the Virgin Mary's Immaculate Conception

R. Be our health and protection.

CHAPLET IN HONOR OF
THE IMMACULATE HEART OF MARY
Suitable for a Novena

V. Incline unto my aid, O God!

R. O Lord, make haste to help me!

V. Glory be to the Father, etc.

R. As it was in the beginning, etc.

1. Immaculate Virgin, who, conceived without sin, didst direct every movement of thy most pure heart to that God Who was ever the object of thy love, and who was ever most submissive to His will, obtain for me the grace to hate sin with my whole heart, and to learn of thee to live in perfect resignation to the will of God.

Our Father (once), Hail Mary (seven times).

Heart transpierced with pain and woe,
Set my heart with love aglow!

2. I marvel, Mary, at thy deep humility, through which thy blessed heart was troubled at the gracious message brought thee by Gabriel, the archangel, that thou wast chosen Mother of the Son of the Most High, and through which thou didst proclaim thyself his humble handmaid. Wherefore, in great confusion at the sight of my pride, I ask thee for the grace of a contrite and humble heart, that, knowing my own misery, I may obtain that crown of glory promised to the truly humble of heart.

Our Father, etc., Heart, etc.

3.　Blessed Virgin, who, in thy sweetest heart, didst keep as a precious treasure the words of Jesus thy Son, and pondering on the lofty mysteries they contained, didst learn to live for God alone, how doth my cold heart confound me! O dearest Mother! Get me grace so to meditate within my heart upon God's holy law that I may strive to follow thee in the fervent practice of every Christian virtue.

Our Father, etc., Heart, etc.

4.　Glorious Queen of martyrs, whose sacred heart was pierced in thy Son's bitter Passion by the sword, whereof the holy man Simeon had prophesied, gain for my heart true courage and a holy patience to bear the troubles and misfortunes of this miserable life, that so by crucifying my flesh with its desires while following the mortification of the Cross, I may indeed show myself to be a true son of thine.

Our Father, etc., Heart, etc.

5.　O Mary, Mystical Rose, whose loving heart, burning with the living fire of charity, did accept us for thy sons at the foot of the Cross, becoming thus our tender Mother, make me feel the sweetness of thy maternal heart and thy power with Jesus, that when menaced by the perils of this mortal life, and most of all in the dread hour of death, my

heart united with thine may love my Jesus then and through all ages. Amen.
Our Father, etc., Heart, etc.

Let us now turn to the Most Sacred Heart of Jesus, that He may inflame us with His holy love!

O Divine Heart of Jesus! To Thee I consecrate myself, full of deep gratitude for the many blessings I have received and daily do receive from Thy boundless charity. With my whole heart I thank thee for having, in addition to them all, vouchsafed to give me Thy own most holy Mother, giving me to her as a son, in the person of the beloved disciple. Let my heart ever burn with love for Thee, finding in Thy sweetest Heart its peace, its refuge, and its happiness.

The Franciscan Crown

THE FRANCISCAN CROWN
or
THE ROSARY OF THE SEVEN JOYS OF THE BLESSED VIRGIN MARY

The Franciscan Rosary of the Seven Joys of the Blessed Virgin Mary is composed of seven decades of one Our Father and ten Hail Marys each. At the end two Hail Marys are added, and it is concluded with the Our Father and Hail Mary. The last Our Father and Hail Mary are said for the intentions of the Pope in order to gain the indulgence. The 72 Hail Marys commemorate the seventy-two years the Blessed Mother is supposed to have lived on earth. The seven decades need not be recited at once, but the single decades may be separated provided that the whole Rosary is said on the same day. It is not necessary to meditate on the mysteries of this Rosary; it suffices to say the single decades in honor of the respective mystery.

The following are the mysteries of the Franciscan Crown:

First Mystery: The Immaculate Virgin Mary joyfully conceived Jesus by the Holy Spirit.

Second Mystery: The Immaculate Virgin Mary joyfully carried Jesus when she went to visit Elizabeth.

Third Mystery: The Immaculate Virgin Mary brought Jesus into the world.

Fourth Mystery: The Immaculate Virgin Mary joyfully exhibited Jesus to the adoration of the Magi.

Fifth Mystery: The Immaculate Virgin Mary joyfully found Jesus in the Temple.

Sixth Mystery: The Immaculate Virgin Mary joyfully beheld Jesus after His Resurrection.

Seventh Mystery: The Immaculate Virgin Mary was joyfully received by Jesus into heaven, and crowned Queen of heaven and earth.

The use of this rosary was begun in the order of St. Francis in 1422. It is said that a certain novice, before joining the Order, was accustomed to place a crown on a statue of the Blessed Virgin. When he was not allowed to continue this practice, he resolved to leave the Order. Then Mary appeared to him and dissuaded him, telling him that he could offer a much more pleasing crown by reciting a rosary of seven decades in honor of her Seven Joys. This is the most highly indulgenced of all the types of rosaries.

THE ROSARY OF THE SEVEN SORROWS

The Rosary of the Seven Sorrows consists of seven groups of seven beads, with three additional beads and a Crucifix. The seven groups of seven Hail Marys are recited in remembrance of the Seven Sorrows of Mary, namely:

1. The prophecy of Simeon.
2. The flight into Egypt.
3. The loss of the Child Jesus in the Temple.
4. Mary meets Jesus carrying His Cross.
5. The Crucifixion.
6. Mary receives the body of Jesus from the Cross.
7. The body of Jesus is placed in the tomb.

Three Hail Marys are added in remembrance of the tears Mary shed because of the suffering of her Divine Son. These are said to obtain true sorrow for our sins. Following is the concluding prayer.

V. Pray for us, O most sorrowful Virgin.

R. That we may be made worthy of the promises of Christ.

Prayer

Lord Jesus, we now implore, both for the present and for the hour of our death, the intercession of the most Blessed Virgin Mary, Thy Mother, whose holy soul was pierced at the time of Thy passion by a sword of grief. Grant us this favor, O Savior of the world, Who livest and reignest with the Father and the Holy Spirit forever and ever. Amen.

The Rosary of the Seven Sorrows

THE LITTLE ROSARY
OF THE SEVEN DOLORS OF MARY

With Meditations by St. Alphonsus Liguori
(optional)

V. Incline unto mine aid, O God.
R. O Lord, make haste to help me.

Glory be to the Father, and to the Son, and to the Holy Ghost; as it was in the beginning, is now, and ever shall be, world without end. Amen.

Strophe:
My Mother, share thy grief with me,
And let me bear thee company
To mourn thy Jesus' death with thee.

Meditations on the First Dolor: I pity thee, O afflicted Mother, on account of the first sword of sorrow which pierced thee, when in the Temple all the outrages which men would inflict on thy beloved Jesus were presented before thee by Saint Simeon, and which thou didst already know by the Sacred Scriptures; outrages which were to cause Him to die before thine eyes, on an infamous Cross, exhausted of His blood, abandoned by all, and thyself unable to defend or help Him. By that bitter knowledge, then, which for so many years afflicted thy heart, I beseech thee, my Queen, to obtain for me the grace that during my life and at death I may ever keep the Passion of Jesus and thy sorrows impressed upon my heart.

Our Father, seven Hail Marys, and the Strophe are repeated after each Dolor.

Meditation on the Second Dolor: I pity thee, my afflicted Mother, for the second sword which pierced thee, when soon after His birth thou didst behold thine innocent Son threatened with death by those very men for whose salvation He had come into the world, so that in the darkness of night thou wast obliged to fly secretly with Him into Egypt. By the many hardships, then, which thou, a delicate young woman, in company with thine exiled Child, didst endure in so long and fatiguing a journey through rough and desert countries, and during thy residence in Egypt, where, being unknown and a stranger, thou didst live for so many years in poverty and contempt, I beseech thee, my beloved Lady, to obtain for me the grace to suffer in thy company with patience until death the trials of this miserable life, that I may thus in the next escape the eternal punishments of Hell, which I have deserved.

Our Father, seven Hail Marys and the Strophe.

Meditation on the Third Dolor: I pity thee, my sorrowful Mother, on account of the third sword which pierced thee in the loss of thy dear Son Jesus, who remained absent from thee in Jerusalem for three days. No longer seeing thy Beloved by thy side and not knowing the cause of His absence, I can well imagine, my loving Queen, that during those nights thou didst not repose and didst only sigh for Him, Who was all thy treasure. By the sighs, then, of those three days, for thee too long and bitter, I beseech thee to obtain for me the grace that I may never lose my God, that so, always clinging to Him, I may leave the world united to Him.

Our Father, seven Hail Marys and the Strophe.

Meditation on the Fourth Dolor: I pity thee, my sorrowful Mother, for the fourth sword which pierced thee in seeing thy Son condemned to death, bound with cords and chains, covered with blood and wounds, crowned with a wreath of thorns, falling under the heavy weight of the Cross which He carried on His wounded shoulders, going as an innocent Lamb to die for love of us. Thine eyes met His, and His met thine; and your glances were as so many cruel arrows which wounded your loving hearts. By this great sorrow, then, I beseech thee to obtain for me the grace to live in all things resigned to the will of my God and to carry my cross cheerfully in company with Jesus, until my last breath.

Our Father, seven Hail Marys and the Strophe.

Meditation on the Fifth Dolor: I pity thee, my afflicted Mother, for the fifth sword which pierced thee, when on Mount Calvary thou didst behold thy beloved Son Jesus slowly dying before thine eyes, amid so many torments and insults, on that hard bed of the Cross, where thou couldst not administer to Him even the least of those comforts which are granted to the greatest criminals at the hour of death. I beseech thee by the agony which thou, my most loving Mother, didst endure, together with thy dying Son, and by the sadness which thou didst feel when, for the last time, He spoke to thee from the Cross and bade thee farewell and left all of us in the person of Saint John to thee as thy children; by that constancy with which thou didst then see Him bow down His head and expire, I beseech thee to obtain for me the grace from thy crucified Love to live and die crucified to all earthly things, that I may spend my life for God alone and thus one day enter Paradise to enjoy Him face to face.

Our Father, seven Hail Marys and the Strophe.

Meditation on the Sixth Dolor: I pity thee, my afflicted Mother, for the sixth sword which pierced thee when thou didst see the sweet Heart of thy Son pierced through and through. He was already dead and had died for those ungrateful creatures who, even after His death, were not satisfied with the torments they had inflicted upon Him. By this cruel sorrow, then which was all thine, I beseech thee to obtain for me the grace to dwell in the Heart of Jesus, wounded and open for me; in that Heart, I say, which is the beautiful abode of love, in which all souls who love God repose; and that, living there, I may never think of or love anything but God. Most sacred Virgin, thou canst obtain this for me; from thee do I hope for it.

Our Father, seven Hail Marys and the Strophe.

Meditation on the Seventh Dolor: I pity thee, my afflicted Mother, for the seventh sword which pierced thee on seeing thy Son already dead in thine arms, no longer fair and beautiful as thou didst receive Him in the stable of Bethlehem, but covered with blood, livid and all lacerated with wounds, so that even His bones were seen; thou didst then say, "My Son, my Son, to what has love reduced Thee!" And when He was borne to the sepulcher, thou wouldst thyself accompany Him and place Him with thine own hands in the tomb; and bidding Him thy last farewell, thou didst leave thy loving heart buried with thy Son. By this martyrdom of thy beautiful soul, do thou obtain for me, O Mother of Fair Love, the forgiveness of the offenses which I have committed against my beloved God, and which I repent with my whole heart. Do thou defend me in temptations; do thou assist me at the moment of my death, that, saving my soul through the merits of Jesus and thee, I may one day, after this miserable exile, go to Paradise to sing the praises of Jesus and of thee for all eternity. Amen.

Our Father, seven Hail Marys and the Strophe.

V. Pray for us, O most sorrowful Virgin,

R. That we may be made worthy of the promises of Christ.

Let us pray.

O Lord, at Whose Passion, according to the prophecy of Simeon, a sword of sorrow didst pierce through the most sweet soul of the glorious Virgin and Mother Mary, grant that we who commemorate and reverence her dolors may experience the blessed effect of Thy Passion, who livest and reignest world without end. Amen.

THE ROSARY OF OUR LADY'S TEARS

Next to the Most Precious Blood of Jesus there is nothing more touching and effective than the tears of our heavenly Mother! How many tears she shed on the way of the Cross and when she stood beneath the Cross! She shed bitter tears in reparation for the many insults her Divine Son received then and which He would receive in the future. She wept bitter tears for the many souls who would not submit to the commandments of God and so would be lost forever.

In recent centuries, too, she wept tears of sorrow. The account of the apparitions of Our Lady of La Salette on September 19, 1846 is very moving, as is also the account of Mary's tears at Syracuse. There the image of Our Lady wept again and again from a simple terra cotta plaque in the house of a poor worker. This occurred from August 29 to September 2, 1953. After a thorough investigation the bishops of Sicily confirmed this a miracle of tears. Hundreds of thousands of people came to see it and Pope Pius XII exclaimed on the radio, "O the tears of Mary!"

The Origin of the Rosary of Tears

This rosary was revealed in 1929 and 1930, that is, over fifty years ago, by the Savior and His most holy Mother to Sister Amalia in Campina (Brazil) and was confirmed as supernatural by Bishop Campos Baretto.

Our Lord's consoling words to Sister Amalia on November 8, 1929 were:

"My daughter, whatever I am asked, through the tears of My Mother I shall give lovingly."

And on March 8, 1930 the most Pure Mother stated:

"Through this rosary the devil will be subdued and the power of hell will be destroyed. Prepare yourself for this great combat."

Why does the devil have such great power today? Because so many no longer believe in him and because sin has become too powerful.

How to Pray The Rosary of Tears

Instead of the Creed say: Crucified Jesus! We fall at your feet and offer you the tears of her who with deep compassionate love accompanied you on your sorrowful way of the Cross. Grant, O good Master, that we take to heart the lessons which the tears of your most holy Mother teach us, so that we may fulfill Your holy will on earth and be worthy to praise and exalt you in Heaven for all eternity.

Instead of the Our Father say:

V. O Jesus, look upon the tears of her who loved you most on earth,
R. And loves you most ardently in Heaven.

Instead of the Hail Mary, say:

V. O Jesus, hear our prayers
R. For the sake of your most holy Mother's tears.

At the end repeat three times on the small beads:

V. O Jesus, look upon the tears of her who loved you most on earth,
R. And loves you most ardently in Heaven."

After the last three invocations say the closing prayer:

O Mary, Mother of love, sorrow and mercy, we beg you to unite your prayers with ours so that Jesus, your Divine Son, to whom we turn, may hear our petitions in the name of your maternal tears and may give us in addition to the favors we ask, the crown of everlasting life. Amen.

The Rosary of the Tears of Blood

THE ROSARY OF THE TEARS OF BLOOD

Begin:

Crucified Jesus, prostrate at Thy feet, we offer to Thee the tears of blood of her who with intimate sympathetic love accompanied Thee on Thy way to Calvary. Grant, O good Master, that we take to heart the lessons which the blood-stained tears of Thy most holy mother afford us, so that we may so fulfill Thy holy will on earth that we may become worthy to laud and praise Thee in heaven for all eternity. Amen.

Seven small rules: Instead of the Our Father one says:

O Jesus, look upon the tears of blood of her who loved Thee most while on earth, and who loves Thee most intimately in heaven.

Instead of the Hail Mary say:

O Jesus, hear our petitions for the sake of the tears of blood shed by Thy dearest mother. *(seven times)*

At the end say three times:

O Jesus, look... and then, O Mary, mother of love, of sorrows, and of mercy, we beg thee, join thy prayers with ours so that Jesus thy divine Son, to whom we turn, will graciously hear our petitions in the name of thy maternal tears of blood, and together with the graces we implore, grant us finally the reward of eternal life. Amen.

Thy tears of blood, O sorrowful mother, destroy the rule of Satan. Through Thy divine tenderness, O bound and fettered Jesus, defend the world from the errors which threaten it. Amen.

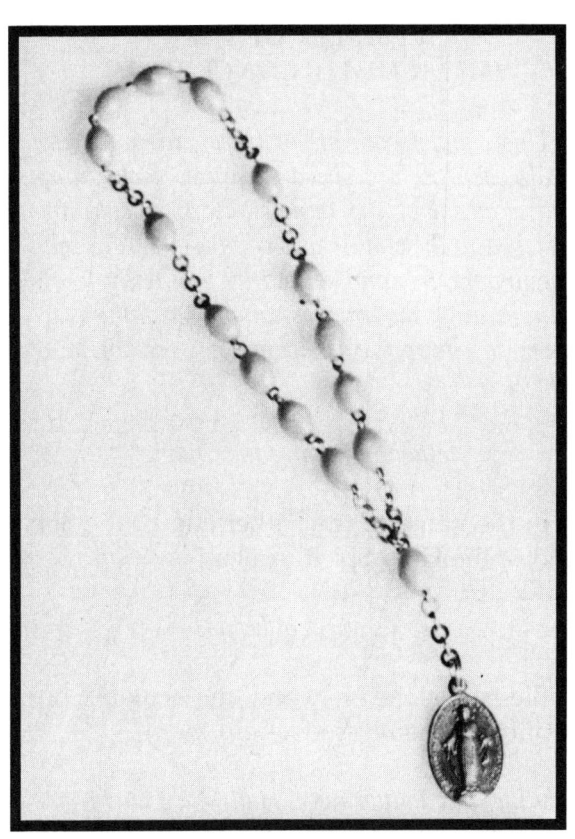

The Chaplet of the Immaculate Conception

CHAPLET OF THE IMMACULATE CONCEPTION

This chaplet consists of three groups of four beads each. A large bead separates each group, and a medal of the Immaculate Conception is attached to the end. It was composed by St. John Berchmans, S.J. and recited by him daily to obtain, through the intercession of Mary, the grace never to commit any sin against the virtue of purity.

Method of Saying the Chaplet

In the name of the Father and of the Son and of the Holy Spirit. Amen.

First set of beads

Blessed be the Holy and Immaculate Conception of the Blessed Virgin Mary.

Say the Our Father once, Hail Mary four times, Glory be to the Father once.

Second set
Same prayers.

Third set
Same prayers.

ROSARY IN PRAISE OF THE MOST BLESSED VIRGIN IN REPARATION FOR BLASPHEMIES

Mary, my Immaculate Mother, I desire to offer you reparation for the offenses which your Immaculate Heart receives from the horrible blasphemies which are uttered against you. I offer you these praises to console you for so many ungrateful children who do not love you, and to console the Heart of your Divine Son who is so deeply offended by the insults offered to you.

Receive, my Purest Mother, this little act of homage. Make me love you more each day and look with pity on those blasphemers that they may not delay to cast themselves into your maternal arms. Amen.

Grant that I may praise you, O Holy Virgin!
Give me strength against your enemies!

1. Blessed be the great Mother of God, Mary Most Holy!
2. Blessed be her Holy and Immaculate Conception!
3. Blessed be her Glorious Assumption!
4. Blessed be the Name of Mary, Virgin and Mother!
5. Blessed be her Immaculate Heart!
6. Blessed be her Virginal Purity!

7. Blessed be her Divine Maternity!
8. Blessed be her Universal Mediation!
9. Blessed be her Sorrows and her Tears!
10. Blessed be the graces with which the Lord crowned her Queen of Heaven and Earth!

Glory be to Mary, Daughter of the Father!
Glory be to Mary, Mother of the Son!
Glory be to Mary, Spouse of the Holy Spirit!

Final Prayer:

My Mother, I love you for those who do not love you; I praise you for those who blaspheme you; I surrender myself to you for those who will not recognize you as their Mother.

(Repeat the praises and final prayer five times.)

The above praises were published in Peru With the Imprimatur of the Archbishop of Lima on October 26, 1953. This translation is offered to help English-speaking people join in this practical form of reparation to the Immaculate Heart of Mary.

CHAPLET OF
OUR LADY OF GUADALUPE

Crucifix – Mystical Rose

Our Lady of Guadalupe, Mystical Rose, make intercession for our Holy Church, protect the sovereign Pontiff, help all those who invoke you in their necessities, and since you are the ever Virgin Mary and Mother of the true God, obtain for us from your most Holy Son the grace of keeping our faith, of sweet hope in the midst of the bitterness of life, of burning charity, and the precious gift of final perseverance. Amen.

Our Father.

Four Hail Marys in honor of her four apparitions to Blessed Juan Diego. Glory Be.

First Apparition: *Our Lady of Guadalupe appears to Blessed Juan Diego. Our Lady requests a temple in her honor.*

Our Father.

Meditation: Our Lady of Guadalupe, my Queen and my Mother, I thank you for your first apparition to Blessed Juan Diego when you revealed that you are the Most Pure Virgin, Mary, Mother of the True God and

Our Lady of Guadalupe Chaplet

Mother of all mankind. I thank you for requesting a temple to be built where you stood, to bear witness to your love, your compassion, your aid and your protection for all who would love you, trust you, and invoke your help.

Three Hail Marys, Glory be.

Second Apparition: *Our Lady of Guadalupe gives Blessed Juan Diego encouragement after his return from the Bishop's house.*

Our Father.

Meditation: Our Lady of Guadalupe, my Queen and my Mother, I thank you for your second apparition to Blessed Juan Diego when, upon his return from the Bishop's house, he knelt in humiliation and defeat before you since he was unable to accomplish your mission. I thank you for the courage and encouragement you gave to Blessed Juan Diego to make a second appeal to the Bishop.

Three Hail Marys, Glory be.

Third Apparition: *Our Lady of Guadalupe promises a sign to Blessed Juan Diego for the Bishop.*

Our Father. 203

Mother, I thank you for your third apparition to Blessed Juan Diego when, after this unsuccessful attempt to have a temple built, you said to him, "So be it, son. Return tomorrow in order that you may secure for the Bishop the sign for which he has asked. When this is in your possession, he will believe you; he will no longer doubt your word and suspect your good faith. Be assured that I shall reward you for all that you have undergone."

Three Hail Marys, Glory be.

Fourth Apparition: *Our Lady of Guadalupe fulfills her promise by showing herself on the tilma of Blessed Juan Diego.*

Our Father.

Meditation: Our Lady of Guadalupe, my Queen and my Mother, I thank you for your fourth apparition to Blessed Juan Diego when you ordered him to pick the roses he would find on the summit of the hill and bring them to you. I thank you for arranging them in his tilma when you said, "This cluster of roses is the sign that you shall take to the Bishop. You are to tell him, in my name, that in this he will recognize my will and that he must fulfill it. You will be my ambassador, wholly worthy of my confidence. Only in the presence of the Bishop shall you unfold your mantle and disclose that which you carry." I thank you for your image printed on the tilma which appeared when the roses were released.

Three Hail Marys, Glory be.

Closing Prayer: Remember, O most gracious Virgin of Guadalupe, that in thy celestial apparition on the Mount of Tepeyac, thou didst promise to show thy compassion and pity towards all who, loving and trusting thee, seek thy help and call upon thee in their necessities and afflictions; also to hearken to our supplications, to dry our tears and to give us consolation and relief.

Inspired with this confidence we come before thy august presence, certain that thou wilt deign to fulfill thy merciful promises. We are full of hope that, standing beneath thy protection nothing will trouble or afflict us. Thou has desired to remain with us through thy admirable image, thou who art our Mother, our health and our life.

O Mary, Mother of God, hear our petitions and in thy mercy answer us. Amen.

PRAYER TO OUR LADY OF GUADALUPE

Our Lady of Guadalupe, my mother, into your hands joined in prayer, take my prayers, petitions and hopes, and present them to Jesus for me.

Remembering the love and care your hands rendered to Him, He will not refuse what they hold now, even though they are from me. Amen.

Our Lady of Consolation Beads

ROSARY OR LITTLE BEADS OF
OUR LADY OF CONSOLATION

This chaplet consists of 13 beads with a medal of St. Augustine. On each bead is said an Our Father and a Hail Mary, and at the end the Hail Holy Queen is recited. The 12 Our Fathers and Hail Marys are in honor of the 12 Apostles; the other Our Father and Hail Mary are in honor of Our Lord, King of the Apostles.

While reciting these prayers one should meditate on the 12 articles of the Apostle's Creed and pray for the safety of our Holy Father, the Pope, and for the welfare of the Church.

This chaplet is designated especially for the Augustinian secular tertiaries.

OUR LADY OF PERPETUAL HELP
ROSARY

On the Crucifix say the
Hail, Holy Queen.

On the large beads say:
Mary can help us,
Mary will help us,
Mary wants to help us,
Mary must help us.

On the small beads say:
Mother of Perpetual Help, pray for us.

End with the Memorare *to Mary.*

CHAPLET OF OUR LADY
STAR OF THE SEA

For Special Needs

Our Lady Star of the Sea, Stella Maris, is the Patroness of the men who sail the seas. Saint Bonaventure reminds us that she also "guides to a landfall in heaven those who navigate the sea of this world in the ship of innocence or penance." Ships at sea might be guided by the North Star. Our Lady, Star of the Sea, aids not only the sailors aboard those ships, she also aids all those who sail the stormy seas of life.

The Medal Prayer:
A Prayer to the Blessed Virgin

Most beautiful Flower of Mount Carmel, Fruitful Vine, Splendor of Heaven, Blessed Mother of the Son of God, Immaculate Virgin, assist me in this my necessity. O Star of the Sea, help me and show me herein you are my Mother.

Holy Mary, Mother of God, Queen of Heaven and Earth, I humbly beseech you from the bottom of my heart, to succor me in this necessity; there are none that can withstand your power.

First Three Beads:

One Our Father, one Hail Mary, one Glory Be on each of the three beads for Bishop Warren Boudreaux, Pope John Paul II and Father John Paul Finke.

On each of the 12 Beads, which represent the 12 Stars of Our Lady's Crown, Pray:
One Hail Mary on each bead and the following invocations:

Our Lady, Star of the Sea, Help and Protect us!

Sweet Mother, I place this cause in your hands.

+Imprimatur: Bishop Warren L. Boudreaux, Bishop of Houma, Thibodaux.

The Confraternity of Our Lady Star of the Sea in Morgan City, Louisiana was established by Bishop Warren L. Boudreaux on August 22, 1979. Those wishing to obtain further information concerning membership may write: The Confraternity of Our Lady Star of the Sea, Central Headquarters, P.O. Box 609, Morgan City, LA 70381.

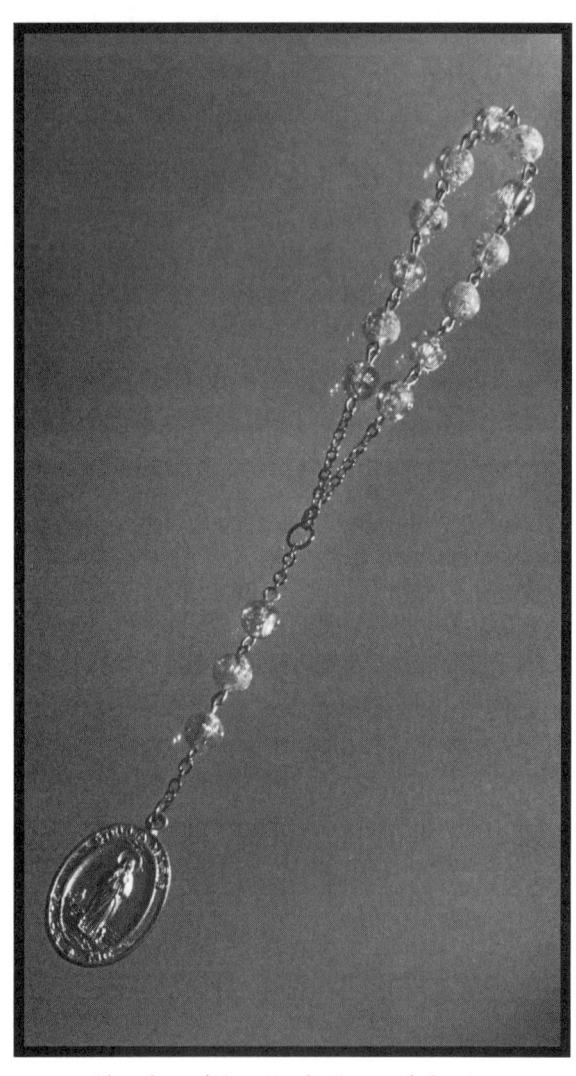

Chaplet of Our Lady Star of the Sea

CHAPLET OF
OUR LADY OF CZESTOCHOWA

O Almighty and merciful God! You gave the Polish Nation a wondrous help and defense in the most holy Virgin Mary and You honored Her sacred image at Jasna Gora with remarkable veneration of the faithful. Grant in Your mercy that, under Her protection, we may struggle confidently throughout our lives and at the moment of death be victorious over our enemy. We ask this through Christ our Lord. Amen.

Lady of Jasna Gora, our Mother, Queen of the Polish Nation! Trusting in Your maternal goodness and powerful intercession with Your Son, we place before You our humble prayers and petitions. To You we commend all our needs, in particular... and all children of the Polish Nation whether in their native land or elsewhere in the world.

Say three Our Fathers, three Hail Marys and three Glorias.

Chaplet of Our Lady of Czestochowa

THE DOMINICAN CHAPLET

The Crucifix:

The Sign of the Cross and the Apostles' Creed.

The White Bead:
Our Father for the intention of the Holy Father.

The Blue Beads:
Five Hail Marys for the Joys of Jesus and Mary.

The Black Beads:
Five Hail Marys for the Sorrows of Jesus and Mary.

The Gold Beads:
Five Hail Marys for the Glories of Jesus and Mary.

The White Bead:
Our Father for the intention of the Master General (all Dominican leaders).

Lord Jesus, moved by the urgent need for Priests, Religious and Apostles, and following your recommendation to pray the Lord of the harvest to send laborers for the salvation of souls, we implore You, through the intercession of our holy Mother Mary, Queen of the Rosary, and through the intercession of our Holy Founder, St. Dominic, to increase in number the members of our Dominican family.

Enlighten their minds, strengthen their wills, aid them to cultivate diligently the divine seed planted in their hearts. Guide them on the upward path of purity that leads to the summit of truth.

Mary, Mother of Mercy, long ago you presented your servant Dominic to Jesus. Now offer your sons and daughters to Him and make them worthy of their sublime mission. Obtain for the Order faithful followers of its religious tradition and numerous apostles after the heart of Dominic. Amen.

The Dominican Chaplet

Chaplet of Conversion

CHAPLET OF CONVERSION

We offer this very beautiful chaplet, requested by Our Blessed Mother, for the conversion of the souls of the world in these times that are serious and urgent. She gave it to a chosen soul in Ireland, but asked that it be prayed widely. It begins:

Say the Creed *for the unbelievers of the world.*

Say one Our Father *in petition to the Father for the grace of conversion for the world.*

Say one Hail Mary, *honoring the Father for the exaltation of Mary, a mere creature, and for choosing to honor her with the title:* Queen of Heaven and Mediatrix of all graces.

Say one Hail, Holy Queen.

Repeat the section below five times.

On the large beads of each mystery say once:

O Holy Mother, I join you at the foot of your Son's Cross to implore mercy and conversion for the souls of the world. With you I offer the wounds of your Son Jesus to the Father in atonement for the sins of the world, past, present and to come.

On the small beads say five times:

Through the sorrowful, bleeding, Immaculate Heart of Mary, and in union with the suffering of her Son Jesus on the Cross, I implore from the Father the grace of conversion for the world.

At the end of each little mystery of five invocations, say one Hail Mary *in honor of Mary's tears of sorrow, followed by this short prayer:*

Holy Mother Mary, Mediatrix of all graces, obtain for us from God the conversion of the world.

At the end of the chaplet say three Glory Be's *in honor of the Blessed Trinity, and conclude with the* Hail, Holy Queen.

The chaplet is made up of a cross, three small beads, and five sets of five small beads separated by five large beads. There are 33 beads in all.

Mother of the Church

St. Michael

222

CHAPLETS OF THE ANGELS

GOD HAS GIVEN HIS ANGELS CHARGE OVER THEE, to KEEP THEE IN ALL THY WAYS. PS. 90

CHAPLET OF THE HOLY ANGELS
(Recited using the Chaplet of St. Michael)

Offering: O my Jesus, I offer this chaplet to Your Divine Heart, that You may render it perfect, thus giving joy to Your holy Angels and so they may keep me under their holy protection, above all at the hour of my death to which I invite them with all my heart. Strengthened by their presence, I will await death with joy and be preserved from the assaults of hell.

I beseech you also, dear Angels, to visit immediately the souls in Purgatory, especially my parents, my friends, my benefactors; help them so that they will soon be delivered. Do not forget me either after my death. This I beg you with all my heart, through the Sacred Heart of Jesus and the Immaculate Heart of Mary. Amen.

1. St. Michael, I recommend the hour of my death to you! Hold the Evil One prisoner, so that he may not battle against me and do harm to my soul.

2. St. Gabriel, obtain for me from God lively faith, strong hope, ardent charity and great devotion to the Blessed Sacrament of the Altar!

3. St. Raphael, lead me constantly on the road of virtue and perfection!

4. My Holy Guardian Angel, obtain for me divine inspiration and the special grace to be faithful!

1. O ardent Seraphim, obtain for me a burning love for God!
One Our Father, three Hail Marys.

2. O Cherubim brilliant with light, obtain for me true knowledge of the science of the saints!
One Our Father, three Hail Marys.

3. O admirable Thrones, obtain for me peace and tranquility of heart!
One Our Father, three Hail Marys.

4. O exalted Dominions, obtain for me victory over all evil thoughts!
One Our Father, three Hail Marys.

5. O invincible Powers, obtain for me strength against all evil spirits!
One Our Father, three Hail Marys.

6. O most serene Virtues, obtain for me obedience and perfect justice!
One Our Father, three Hail Marys.

7. O Principalities, who accomplish prodigies, obtain for me plenitude of all virtue and perfection!
One Our Father, three Hail Marys.

8. O holy Archangels, obtain for me conformity to the Will of God!
One Our Father, three Hail Marys.

9. O holy Angels, O faithful Guardian Angels, obtain for me true humility and great confidence in the divine mercy!
One Our Father, three Hail Marys.

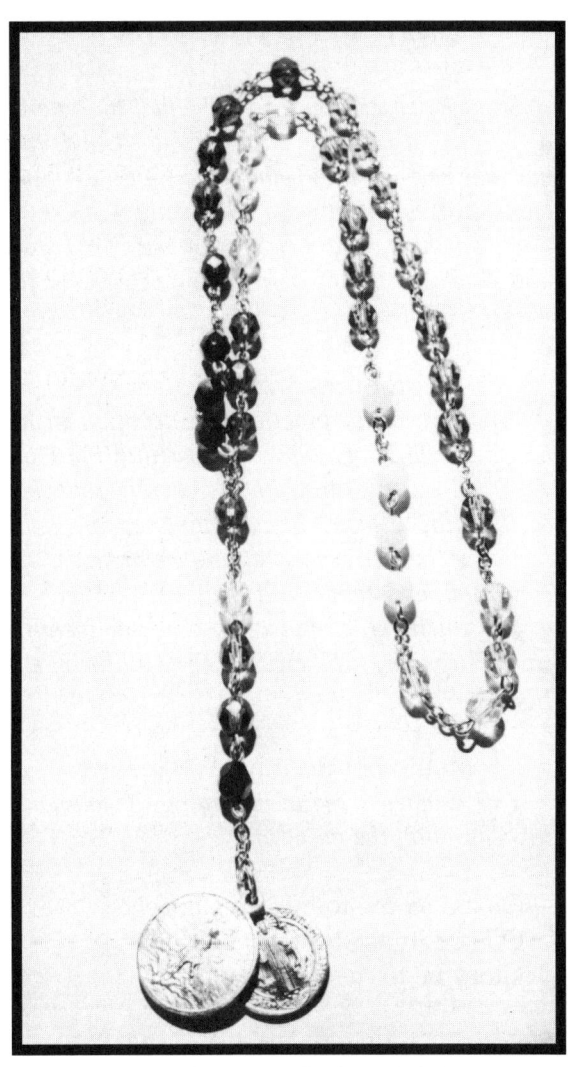

The Chaplet of St. Michael

CHAPLET OF ST. MICHAEL

Saint Michael, appearing one day to Antonia d'Astonac, a most devout Servant of God, told her that he wished to be honored by nine salutations corresponding to the nine Choirs of Angels, which should consist of one Our Father and three Hail Marys in honor of each of the Angelic Choirs.

Promises of St. Michael
Whoever would practice this devotion in his honor would have, when approaching the Holy Table, an escort of nine angels chosen from each of the nine Choirs. In addition, for the daily recital of these nine salutations, he promised his continual assistance and that of all the holy angels during life, and after death deliverance from Purgatory for themselves and all their relations.

Method of Reciting the Chaplet
This chaplet is begun by saying the following invocation on the medal:

O God, come to my assistance!
O Lord, make haste to help me!
Glory be to the Father, etc.

Say one Our Father and three Hail Marys after each of the following nine salutations in honor of the nine Choirs of Angels:

1.

By the intercession of St. Michael and the celestial Choir of Seraphim, may the Lord make us worthy to burn with the fire of perfect charity. Amen.

2.

By the intercession of St. Michael and the celestial Choir of Cherubim, may the Lord vouchsafe to grant us grace to leave the ways of wickedness to run in the paths of Christian perfection. Amen.

3.

By the intercession of St. Michael and the celestial Choir of Thrones, may the Lord infuse into our hearts a true and sincere spirit of humility. Amen.

4.

By the intercession of St. Michael and the celestial Choir of Dominions, may the Lord give us grace to govern our senses and subdue our unruly passions. Amen.

5.

By the intercession of St. Michael and the celestial Choir of Powers, may the Lord vouchsafe to protect our souls against the snares and temptations of the devil. Amen.

6.

By the intercession of St. Michael and the celestial Choir of Virtues, may the Lord preserve us from evil and suffer us not to fall into temptation. Amen.

7.

By the intercession of St. Michael and the celestial Choir of Principalities, may God fill our souls with a true spirit of obedience. Amen.

8.

By the intercession of St. Michael and the celestial Choir of Archangels, may the Lord give us perseverance in faith and in all good works, in order that we gain the glory of Paradise. Amen.

9.

By the intercession of St. Michael and the celestial Choir of Angels, may the Lord grant us to be protected by them in this mortal life and conducted hereafter to eternal glory. Amen.

Say one Our Father in honor of each of the following leading Angels: St. Michael, St. Gabriel, St. Raphael, our Guardian Angel.

The chaplet is concluded with the following prayers:

O glorious prince St. Michael, chief and commander of the heavenly hosts, guardian of souls, vanquisher of rebel spirits, servant in the house of the Divine King and our admirable conductor, thou who dost shine with excellence and superhuman virtue, vouchsafe to deliver us from all evil, who turn to thee with confidence, and enable us by thy gracious protection to serve God more and more faithfully every day.

V. Pray for us, O glorious St. Michael, Prince of the Church of Jesus Christ!

R. That we may be made worthy of His promises!

Prayer

Almighty and Everlasting God, who by a prodigy of goodness and a merciful desire for the salvation of all men hast appointed the most glorious Archangel St. Michael Prince of Thy Church, make us worthy, we beseech Thee, to be delivered from all our enemies, that none of them may harass us at the hour of death, but that we may be conducted by him into the august presence of Thy Divine Majesty. This we beg through the merits of Jesus Christ our Lord. Amen.

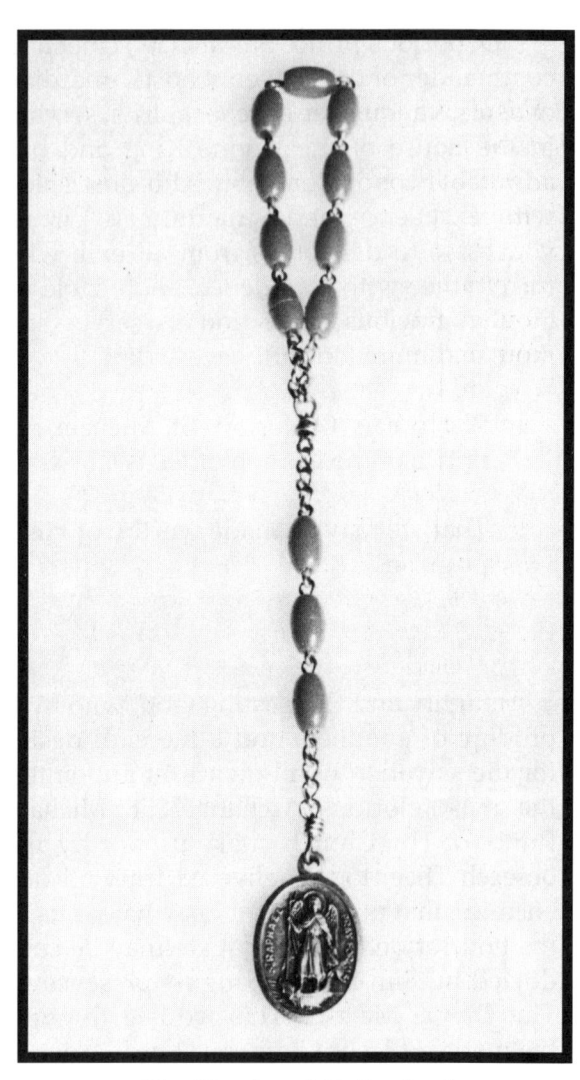

The Chaplet of St. Raphael

CHAPLET OF ST. RAPHAEL

This chaplet consists of a medal of St. Raphael, three beads in honor of Mary, Queen of Angels, and nine beads in honor of the nine Angelic Choirs.

On the medal say:
You are Raphael the Healer,
You are Raphael the Guide,
You are Raphael the Companion,
Ever at Human Sorrow's side.

On the small beads say three Hail Marys to Mary, Queen of Angels.
On then nine beads say the following prayer, once in honor of each of the nine Angelic Choirs (Angels, Archangels, Principalities, Powers, Virtues, Dominions, Thrones, Cherubim and Seraphim):
Holy, holy, holy, Lord God of Hosts,
Heaven and earth are full of Your Glory.
Glory be to the Father; Glory be to the Son;
Glory be to the Holy Spirit.

Concluding Aspiration:
St. Raphael, Angel of health, of love, of joy and light, pray for us!

CHAPLET TO THE ARCHANGEL GABRIEL

This chaplet, which consists of a medal of St. Gabriel and 33 beads, was composed by Clare Barros of Foxboro, Massachusetts, to complete the chaplets to the Archangels. It is used here with her permission.

Heavenly Father, through the salutation of the Archangel Gabriel, may we honor the Incarnation of Your Divine Son.

Mother of our Savior, may we strive always to imitate your holy virtues and to respond to our Father... "Be it done unto me according to Thy Word."

Archangel Gabriel, please praise our Father for the gift of His Son—praying, one day, by His grace, we may all be one.

On the three sets of 11 beads we pray:
Hail, full of grace, The Lord is with Thee: Blessed art thou among women.

On the two center beads which join the three sets of 11 we pray:
Behold thou shalt conceive in thy womb, and shalt bring forth a son: and thou shalt call his name Jesus.

Chaplet to the Archangel Gabriel

The three sets of 11 beads total 33 beads in honor of the 33 years of Our Savior's life.

The two joining beads honor the Divinity and the Humanity of Jesus.

"With Ecclesiastical Approval"
Bernard Cardinal Law 10/22/92

NOVENA IN HONOR OF THE NINE CHOIRS OF ANGELS

This Novena has proven to be highly effective in times of stress or emergency.

Glory be to the Father, and to the Son, and to the Holy Spirit,

As it was in the beginning, is now, and ever shall be, world without end. Amen.

Repeat the Glory be to the Father nine times in honor of the Nine Choirs of Angels, nine times during the day.

This novena has been made into a chaplet consisting of 81 beads divided by nine and attached with a medal of Saint Michael.

St. Therese

CHAPLETS OF THE SAINTS

Heart of Jesus, heart divine

All praise, all Thanksgiving

Be every moment thine!

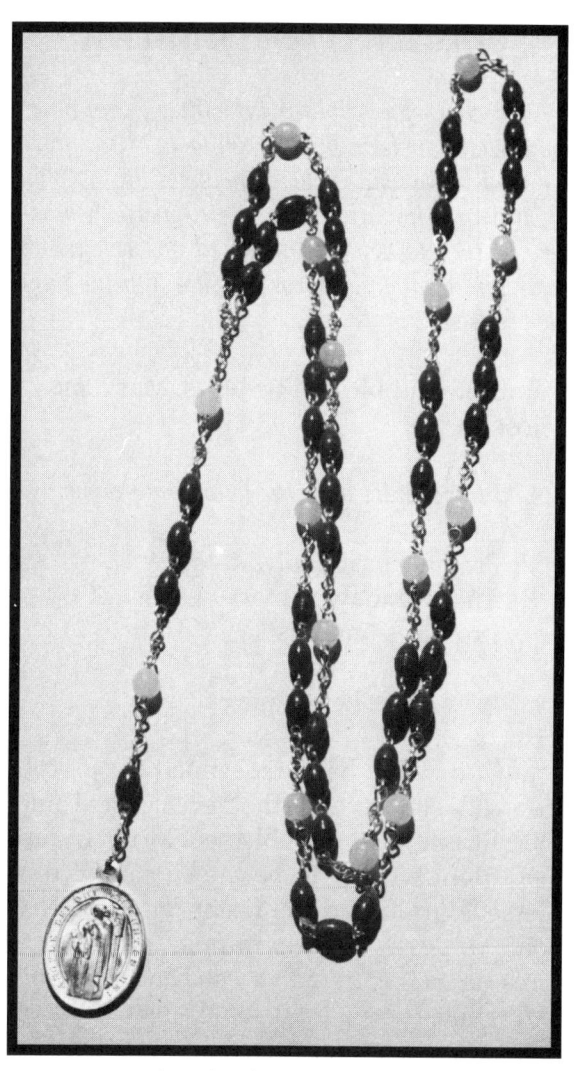

The Chaplet of St. Joseph

THE CHAPLET OF ST. JOSEPH

This chaplet is divided into fifteen groups of four beads consisting of one white and three purple beads. The white bead symbolizes St. Joseph's purity, and the purple his saintly piety. A mystery of the Rosary is considered on each white bead, and two Hail Marys are said. On the purple beads say:

Praised and blessed be Jesus, Mary and Joseph!

End the chaplet with the following prayer:

V. Pray for us, O holy St. Joseph!
R. That we may be made worthy of the promises of Christ!

Let us pray

O God, Who has predestined St. Joseph from all eternity for the service of Thine Eternal Son and His Blessed Mother, and made him worthy to be the spouse of this Blessed Virgin and the foster father of Thy Son: we beseech Thee, through all the services he has rendered to Jesus and Mary on earth, that Thou wouldst make us worthy of his intercession and grant us to enjoy the happiness of his company in heaven. Through Christ our Lord. Amen.

ROSARY IN HONOR OF ST. JOSEPH

On the Crucifix:

O Lord, in order to honor St. Joseph as he deserves, You have taken him body and soul to Heaven to crown him with glory, thus signifying to the world, both visible and invisible, that You have made Joseph Your foster father, the supreme steward of all Your possessions.

On the Large Beads:

We beseech Thee, O Lord, that we may find aid in the merits of the Spouse of Thy Most Holy Mother, so that what we cannot obtain by ourselves may be given us through his intercession, who livest and reignest with God the Father in the unity of the Holy Ghost, one God forever and ever. Amen.

On the Small Beads:

Hail Joseph, Son of David, thou whose holiness surpasses that of all angels and saints, blessed art thou amongst men, thou who wert chosen to be the Spouse of the Blessed Virgin Mary of whom was born Jesus.

Glorious Saint Joseph, now reigning body and soul in Heaven, protector of the Universal Church, pray for us poor sinners now and at the hour of our death. Amen.

THE ROSARY OF SAINT JOSEPH

This Rosary, composed of nine mysteries in all, is divided into 3 parts, each part consisting of 3 decades, in honor of the 30 years that St. Joseph passed in the society of Jesus and Mary.

Mysteries of the First Part

The Incarnation.

The Perplexity of St. Joseph (as to whether he should abandon his Virgin Spouse).

The Birth of Our Lord Jesus Christ in Bethlehem.

Mysteries of the Second Part

The Presentation of the Infant Jesus in the Temple.

The Flight of the Holy Family into Egypt.

The Finding of the Child Jesus in the Temple.

Mysteries of the Third Part

The Hidden Life of Jesus at Nazareth.

The death of St. Joseph.

The Coronation of St. Joseph in Heaven.

(Finish each decade with a Glory Be.)

(Like the Rosary of the Blessed Virgin, one part of the St. Joseph Rosary may be said each day.)

Practice (To conclude the Rosary):

Make three Acts of Contrition, *and beg St. Joseph to obtain for you Pardon and Mercy.*

The St. Joseph Cord

THE ST. JOSEPH CORD

Recite daily in honor of St. Joseph the Glory be to the Father seven times, together with the following prayer:

O St. Joseph, Father and Protector of Virgins, to whose faithful custody Christ Jesus, Innocence itself, and Mary, Virgin of Virgins, were committed; I pray and beseech thee by these dear pledges, Jesus and Mary, that being preserved from all uncleanness, I may with spotless mind, pure heart and chaste body ever more chastely serve Jesus and Mary all the days of my life. Amen.

THE BLESSED CORD OF ST. JOSEPH

Devotion to the Cord of St. Joseph originated in the city of Antwerp, Belgium, in the year 1657. A sister of the Order of St. Augustine, being dangerously ill and about to die, petitioned St. Joseph to cure her. To obtain this favor, the sister placed about her waist a cord which had been blessed, and knotted seven times in honor of the seven sorrows and seven joys of St. Joseph. While wearing the Cord and praying with great fervor and confidence, the sister found herself instantly and completely restored to health.

This miracle was the first of many gained by persons who wore the Cord in honor of St. Joseph and asked his aid in spiritual and temporal necessities. The Holy Father, Pope Pius IX, several times richly blessed this devotion with indulgences and recommended its use. Especially promised to those persons who wear the Cord are the following spiritual benefits:

1) Preservation or recovery of Chastity through St. Joseph's intercession.
2) His special protection during life.
3) His particular assistance at the hour of death.
4) Grace of final perseverance.

The Seven Sorrows of Saint Joseph

1. The doubt of St. Joseph *(Matthew 1,19)*.
2. The birth of Jesus in poverty *(Luke 2,7)*.
3. The circumcision *(Luke 2,21)*.
4. The prophecy of Simeon that many would be lost *(Luke 2,34)*.
5. The flight into Egypt *(Matthew 2,14)*.
6. The return from Egypt *(Matthew 2,22)*.
7. The loss of the Child Jesus *(Luke 2, 45)*.

The Seven Joys of Saint Joseph

1. The message of the Angel *(Matthew 1,20)*.
2. The birth of the Savior *(Luke 2,7)*.
3. The holy name of Jesus *(Matthew 1,25)*.
4. The effects of the Redemption *(Luke 2,34)*.
5. The overthrow of the idols of Egypt *(Isaiah 19,1)*.
6. The life with Jesus and Mary at Nazareth *(Luke 2,39)*.
7. The finding of the Child Jesus in the Temple *(Luke 2,46)*.

THE CHAPLET OF ST. JOSEPH

Say this chaplet on your Rosary beads.

On the Crucifix make the Sign of the Cross and say the Apostles' Creed.

On the large bead say the Our Father.

On the small beads say the Hail, Holy Joseph:

Hail, holy Joseph, spouse of the ever virgin Mary, foster father of God the Son, whom our Father in heaven chose to be head of the Holy Family, pray for us sinners now and at the hour of our death. Amen.

After each set of small beads say the Glory be to the Father and the Fatima prayer.

After five decades say the Memorare of St. Joseph:

Remember, most pure spouse of Mary ever Virgin, my loving protector St. Joseph, that never has it been heard that anyone invoked your protection or besought your aid without being consoled. In this conficonfidence I come before you; I fervently recommend myself to you. Despise not my prayer, Foster Father of the Redeemer, but graciously deign to hear it. Amen.

The Joyful Mysteries

1. **The Annunciation of Joseph.** *The angel of the Lord appears to Joseph in a dream saying, "Joseph, son of David, fear not to take unto yourself Mary your wife, for that which is conceived in her, is of the Holy Spirit." (Mt. 1,20).*

2. **The Birth of Jesus.** *"And she brought forth her firstborn Son." (Lk. 2,7). Joseph glorifies God.*

3. **The Circumcision and Naming of Jesus.** *"Joseph, son of David . . . you shall call His name Jesus, for He shall save His people from their sins." (Mt. 1,20-21).*

4. **The Presentation of the baby Jesus in the Temple.** *"A light to the revelation of the Gentiles, and the glory of Your people Israel. . . And Joseph and His mother were wondering at those things which were spoken concerning Him." (Lk. 2,32-33).*

5. **The Finding of the boy Jesus in the Temple.** *"And when Mary and Joseph saw Him in the temple, they were amazed . . . And He went down with them to Nazareth and was subject to them." (Lk. 2,48;51).*

The Sorrowful Mysteries

1. **Joseph's spouse Mary is found to be with child.** "Joseph, her husband, being a just man, and not willing publicly to expose her, was minded to put her away privately." (Mt. 1,18-19).

2. **The Journey to Bethlehem.** Mary, wife of Joseph, was great with child. . . and there was no room for them in the inn." (Lk. 2,5-7).

3. **Joseph flees to Egypt with Mary and Jesus.** "an angel of the Lord appeared in sleep to Joseph saying: Arise, and take the child and His mother, and fly into Egypt." (Mt. 2,13).

4. **Jesus is lost in Jerusalem.** When Joseph and Mary returned to Nazareth, "the child Jesus remained in Jerusalem; and His parents knew it not." (Lk. 2,43).

5. **The Death of Joseph.** Having faithfully fulfilled his role in God's providence, Joseph expires in the presence of Jesus and Mary.

The Glorious Mysteries

1. ***The Glorification of St. Joseph.*** *Joseph accompanies Jesus after His resurrection to share in Jesus' glory for all eternity and become our intercessor.*

2. ***St. Joseph, Patron of the Universal Church.*** *As he once cherished, nurtured and protected the Son of God, St. Joseph now continues his guidance and protection of His Mystical Body on earth, the Church.*

3. ***St. Joseph, Protector of Families.*** *As head of the Holy Family, St. Joseph blesses and intercedes for all Christian families that they also may become holy families in the sight of God.*

4. ***St. Joseph, Patron of the Sick and Suffering.*** *St. Joseph is the faithful advocate before Jesus for all those in suffering and misfortune who call upon him.*

5. ***St. Joseph, Patron of a Holy Death.*** *As he died in the presence and care of Jesus and Mary, St. Joseph will obtain for us that same blessed privilege at our passage from this life to eternity.*

THE CHAPLET TO ST. PAUL

1. I bless You, O Jesus, for the great mercy granted to St. Paul in changing him from a bold persecutor to an ardent apostle of the Church. And you, O great Saint, obtain for me a heart docile to grace, conversion from my principal defect and total configuration with Jesus Christ.

Jesus, Master, Way, Truth and Life, have mercy on us!

Queen of Apostles, pray for us!

St. Paul the Apostle, pray for us!

2. I bless You, O Jesus, for having elected the Apostle Paul as a model and preacher of holy virginity. And you, O St. Paul, my dear father, guard my mind, my heart and my senses in order that I may know, love and serve only Jesus, and employ all my energies for His glory.

Jesus, Master, Way, Truth and Life, have mercy on us!

Queen of Apostles, pray for us!

St. Paul the Apostle, pray for us!

3. I bless You, O Jesus, for having given through St. Paul examples and teachings of perfect obedience. And you, O great Saint, obtain for me a humble docility to all my superiors, for I am sure that in obedience I shall be victorious over my enemies.

Jesus, Master, Way, Truth and Life, have mercy on us!

Queen of Apostles, pray for us!
St. Paul the Apostle, pray for us!

4. I bless You, O Jesus, for having taught me, by the deeds and by the words of St. Paul, the true spirit of poverty. And you, O great Saint, obtain for me the evangelical spirit of poverty, so that after having imitated you in life, I may be your companion in heavenly glory.

Jesus, Master, Way, Truth and Life, have mercy on us!

Queen of Apostles, pray for us!
St. Paul the Apostle, pray for us!

5. I bless You, O Jesus, for having given to St. Paul a heart so full of love for God and for the Church, and for having saved so many souls through his zeal. And you, our friend, obtain for me an ardent desire to carry out the apostolate of the media of social communication, of prayer, of example, of activity and of word, so that I may merit the reward promised to good apostles.

Jesus, Master, Way, Truth and Life, have mercy on us!

Queen of Apostles, pray for us!
St. Paul the Apostle, pray for us!

The Chaplet of St. Anthony

THE CHAPLET OF ST. ANTHONY

This chaplet is composed of thirteen decades of three beads each. On the first bead of each decade say the Our Father, on the second the Hail Mary, and on the third the Glory be to the Father. At the end recite the Miraculous Responsory.

The Miraculous Responsory
by St. Bonaventure

If miracles thou fain would see,
Lo, error, death, calamity.
The leprous stain, the demon flies,
From beds of pain the sick arise.

The hungry seas forego their prey,
The prisoner's cruel chains give way;
While palsied limbs and chattels lost
Both young and old recovered boast.

And perils perish, plenty's hoard,
Is heaped on hunger's famished board;
Let those relate who know it well,
Let Padua of her patron tell.

The hungry seas, etc.

Glory be to the Father, and to the Son, and to the Holy Spirit.

The hungry seas, etc.

V. Pray for us, blessed Anthony,

R. That we may be made worthy of the promises of Christ.

Let us Pray

O God, let the votive commemoration of Blessed Anthony, Thy confessor, be a source of joy to Thy Church, that she may always be fortified with spiritual assistance, and may deserve to possess eternal joy. Through Christ our Lord. Amen.

Prayer to Obtain from St. Anthony the Restoration of Things that are Lost

Great St. Anthony, who hast received from God a special power to recover lost things, help me that I may find that which I am now seeking. Obtain for me, also, an active faith, perfect docility to the inspirations of grace, disgust for the vain pleasures of the world, and an ardent desire for the imperishable goods of an everlasting happiness. Amen.

ANOTHER METHOD OF RECITING THE
13-BEAD ST. ANTHONY CHAPLET

In addition to the 13 Our Fathers, Hail Marys and Glory be to the Fathers, you may meditate on the following 13 petitions:

1. St. Anthony, who raised the dead, pray for those Christians now in their agony, and for our dear departed.

2. St. Anthony, zealous preacher of the Gospel, fortify us against the errors of the enemies of God, and pray for the Holy Father and the Church.

3. St. Anthony, powerful with the Heart of Jesus, preserve us from the calamities which threaten us on account of our sins.

4. St. Anthony, who drivest away devils, make us triumph over their snares.

5. St. Anthony, lily of heavenly purity, purify us from the stains of the soul and preserve our bodies from all dangers.

6. St. Anthony, healer of the sick, cure our diseases and preserve us in health.

7. St. Anthony, guide of travelers, bring to safe harbor those who are in danger of perishing and calm the troubled waves of passion which agitate our souls.

8. St. Anthony, liberator of captives, deliver us from the captivity of evil.

9. St. Anthony, who restorest to young and old the use of their limbs, obtain for us the perfect use of the senses of our body and the faculties of our soul.

10. St. Anthony, finder of lost things, help us to find all that we have lost in the spiritual and temporal order.

11. St. Anthony, protected by Mary, avert the dangers which threaten our body and our soul.

12. St. Anthony, helper of the poor, help us in our needs and give bread and work to those who ask.

13. St. Anthony, we thankfully proclaim thy miraculous power, and we beseech thee to protect us all the days of our life. Amen.

Behold the Cross of the Lord!
Fly, ye hostile powers!
The Lion of the Tribe of Juda, the root of David, has conquered, Alleluia, Alleluia!

V. Saint Anthony, vanquisher of demons, pray for us!
R. That we may be made worthy of the promises of Christ!

Let us Pray

Grant, O Lord, to Thy people through the intercession of Thy servant, blessed Anthony, the grace to prevail over the powers of darkness, through Christ, our Lord. Amen.

From the snares of the devil deliver us, Saint Anthony.

CHAPLET OF SAINT PATRICK

Prayer on the Medal:
The Apostle's Creed.

On Each of the Twelve Green Beads:
Glory be to the Father, and to the Son, and to the Holy Spirit, as it was in the beginning, is now, and ever shall be, world without end. Amen.

Intention:
Through the intercession of St. Patrick, may God Almighty strengthen our faith, and grant the grace of faith for others.

BREASTPLATE OF ST. PATRICK

Christ as a light,
Illumine and guide me!
Christ as a shield, o'ershadow and cover me!
Christ be under me! Christ be over me!
Christ be beside me, On the left hand and on the right!
Christ be before me, behind me, about me!
Christ this day be within and without me!

from Hymn Before Tara

THE CHAPLET OF ST. JUDE

O Holy St. Jude, Apostle and Martyr, great in virtue and rich in miracles, near kinsman of Jesus Christ, faithful intercessor of all who invoke your special help in time of need. To you I have recourse from the depth of my heart and humbly request assistance. Help me in my present and urgent petition. In return, I promise to make your name known and cause you to be invoked.

Say three Our Fathers, three Hail Marys and three Glorias.

This novena, if said in good faith, has never been known to fail. It must be said for nine consecutive days.

The Chaplet of St. Jude

ST. JUDE 40-BEAD CHAPLET

This chaplet is green and is prayed as follows:

St. Jude, glorious Apostle, faithful servant and friend of Jesus, the name of the traitor has caused you to be forgotten by many, but the true Church invokes you universally as the Patron of things despaired of; pray for me, that finally I may receive the consolation and the succor of Heaven in all my necessities, tribulations and sufferings, particularly *(here make your request),* and that I may bless God with you and all the elect throughout eternity. Amen.

A Hail Mary is recited on each bead with the following invocation:

St. Jude, Apostle, martyr and relative of Our Lord Jesus Christ, of Mary and of Joseph, intercede for us.

The chaplet ends with the following prayer:

O Holy St. Jude, Apostle and martyr, great in virtue and rich in miracles, near kinsman of Jesus Christ, faithful intercessor of all who invoke your special patronage in time of need, to you I have recourse from the depth of my heart and humbly beg you, to whom God has given such great power, to come to my assistance. Help me in my present and urgent petition. In return I promise to make your name known and cause you to be invoked. St. Jude, pray for us and all who invoke your aid. Amen.

The Rosary of St. Anne

ROSARY OF ST. ANNE

This little chaplet dates back to 1875. The author is unknown. This chaplet is the source of a great number of favors both spiritual and temporal.

The chaplet consists of the recitation of the following prayers:

1. *In honor of Jesus, say one Our Father and five Hail Marys.*
   After each Hail Mary say:
   Jesus, Mary and St. Anne, grant the favor I ask.

2. *In honor of Mary, say one Our Father and five Hail Marys.*
   After each Hail Mary say:
   Jesus, Mary and St. Anne, grant the favor I ask.

3. *In honor of St. Anne, say one Our Father and five Hail Marys.*
   After each Hail Mary say:
   Jesus, Mary and St. Anne, grant the favor I ask.

SAINT GERTRUDE CHAPLET

Our Lord told St. Gertrude the Great that the following prayer would release 1,000 souls from Purgatory each time it is said. The prayer was extended to include living sinners as well.

(Note: In one Rosary of this chaplet the prayer is said 50 times!)

Say this chaplet on regular Rosary beads. Begin with the Apostles' Creed, one Our Father, three Hail Marys and a Glory be to the Father.

On each large bead say the Our Father.

On each small bead say the following prayer:

Eternal Father, I offer Thee the Most Precious Blood of Thy Divine Son, Jesus, in union with the Masses said throughout the world today, for all the holy souls in Purgatory, for sinners everywhere, for sinners in the universal Church, those in my own home, and within my family. Amen.

At the end of each decade say:

Most Sacred Heart of Jesus, open the hearts and minds of sinners to the truth and light of God, the Father.

Immaculate Heart of Mary, pray for the conversion of sinners and the world.

Glory be to the Father, and to the Son, and to the Holy Spirit, as it was in the beginning, is now, and ever shall be, world without end. Amen.

Repeat the above prayers for each decade, begin-ning with an Our Father on the large beads.

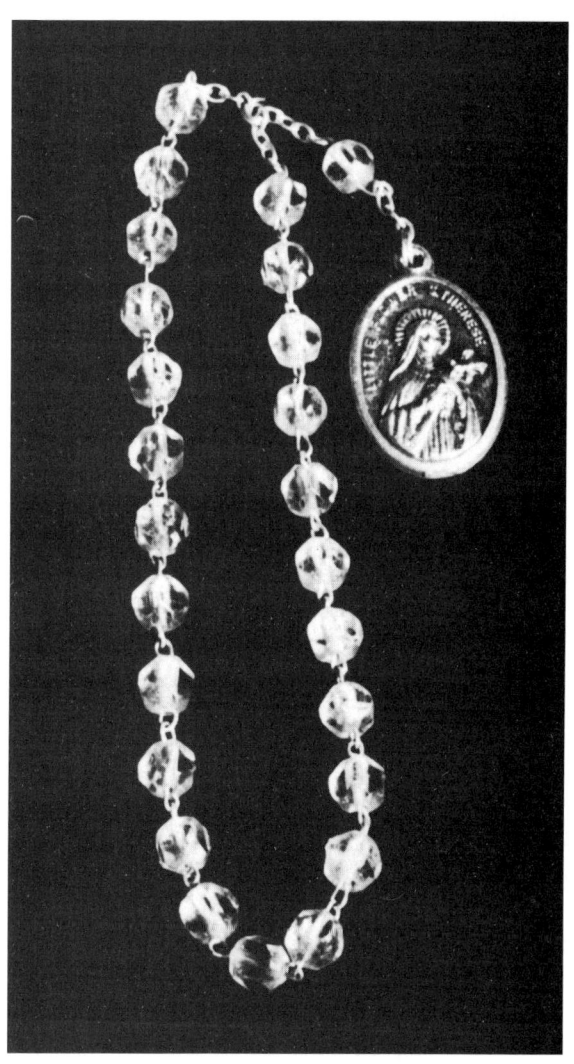

The Little Flower Rosary

271

THE LITTLE FLOWER ROSARY

It is commonly believed that St. Therese grants the sign of a rose to those who practice this devotion during a period of nine to twenty-four days, as a proof that the petition is granted. The sign of a rose or some other visible sign is not always evident, but many persons have received special graces by reciting this chaplet.

To pray this Rosary, bless yourself and say on the first bead:

St. Therese of the Infant Jesus, Patroness of Missions, pray for us!

On each of the remaining twenty-four beads say the Glory be to the Father in honor of the Blessed Trinity, in thanksgiving for giving the world the Little Saint who lived only twenty-four years.

Prayer to St. Therese

St. Therese, the Little Flower, please pick me a rose from the heavenly garden and send it to me with a message of love. Ask God to grant me the favor I thee implore and tell Him I will love Him each day more and more.

(The prayer above, plus five Our Fathers, five Hail Marys and five Glory be to the Fathers, must be said on five successive days before 11 a.m. On the fifth day, when the fifth set of prayers have been completed, offer one more set — five Our Fathers, five Hail Marys and five Glory be to the Fathers.) 272

ST. PHILOMENA CHAPLET

This chaplet consists of three white beads and thirteen red beads. On the medal say the Apostles' Creed to ask for the grace of faith.

On each of the white beads say an Our Father in honor of the three Divine Persons of the Blessed Trinity in thanksgiving for all favors obtained through St. Philomena's intercession.

On each of the red beads, which are thirteen in number to commemorate the thirteen years that St. Philomena spent on earth, say the following prayer:

Hail, O holy St. Philomena, whom I acknowledge, after Mary, as my advocate with the Divine Spouse, intercede for me now and at the hour of my death.

St. Philomena, beloved daughter of Jesus and Mary, pray for us who have recourse to thee. Amen.

In conclusion say:

Hail, O illustrious St. Philomena, who shed so courageously your blood for Christ! I bless the Lord for all the graces He has bestowed upon thee during thy life, and especially at thy death.

The Chaplet of St. Philomena

I praise and glorify Him for the honor and power with which He has crowned thee, and I beg thee to obtain for me from God the graces I ask through thy intercession.

St. Philomena is a most powerful helper of students at examinations.

She cures the sick in the most desperate cases.

She obtains great help for mothers at child-birth.

CHAPLET OF ST. DYMPHNA

This chaplet in honor of St. Dymphna is made up of 17 beads, 15 for the 15 years of her life and 2 for the Holy Father's intentions. This chaplet comes in red, white or green. The red chaplet is recited in honor of her martyrdom, the white in honor of her virginity, and the green for the hope of relief of emotional disorders.

1st bead: Say an Our Father.

2nd bead: Say a Hail Mary for the Holy Father's intentions.

15 beads: Say a Glory be to the Father on each bead in honor of the 15 years of St. Dymphna's life.

Intentions may be made at the beginning or end of the chaplet.

THE LITTLE ROSARY OF
SAINT FRANCES XAVIER CABRINI

Beloved Mother Cabrini was noted for her persistence, both in prayer and in carrying to fulfillment the works of her religious Order. This quality is recommended to those who seek her aid.

The medal of the Little Rosary carries her likeness. On the reverse is seen the Sacred Heart, to which she had great devotion; a pair of wings, her private symbol of the spiritual life; and the Crucifix, of which she has said: "My book will be the Crucifix. I will always keep it before my eyes to learn how to love and to suffer."

Despite discomfort arid inconvenience, Mother Cabrini crossed the ocean twenty-five times, in furtherance of her works. As a notation of this, the Little Rosary contains twenty-five beads.

It is suggested to those using the Little Rosary in her honor to repeat on each bead the Hail Mary and to say after each five beads this aspiration:

O my Savior, hear Saint Frances Xavier Cabrini plead for me.

Little Rosary of St. Frances Xavier Cabrini

Saint Charbel, Wonder Worker of the East

CHAPLET OF ST. CHARBEL

Saint Charbel (or Sharbel) was a Maronite monk from Lebanon. He was born May 8, 1828, ordained a priest July 23, 1859, and died December 24, 1898. He was beatified December 5, 1965 and canonized October 9, 1977.

In the first centuries of Christianity, the Middle East was populated by monks and religious. The Maronite order in particular is known for its love of the monastic life. Out of this tradition God raised up the humble monk Charbel as a light to the whole Church. Charbel is known for his fidelity to his vows, his love for the Eucharist, and his devotion to Our Blessed Mother.

Saint Charbel suffered a stroke while saying Mass the day before Christmas. He was reciting the prayer from the Maronite Mass, **Father of Truth.** *He continued to recite this prayer and to repeat over and over Jesus and Mary until he died several hours later.*

After the death of Charbel, a light began to shine from his tomb attracting the local villagers. Miracles of healing began to take place. Four months after his death his body was exhumed and found to be incorrupt and floating in water. His body remained incorrupt, perspiring blood and liquid until the day of his beatification. Miracles are occurring through the intercession of Saint Charbel to this day.

THE CHAPLET

The chaplet is made up of five sets of beads, three red, one white and one blue. Five black beads divide the sets. A medal of the saint connects the beads, with a single white bead following the medal and preceding the five sets.

The red beads are for the vows of poverty, chastity and obedience, the virtues by which religious share in the Passion of Christ.

The white beads represent the Holy Eucharist, and the blue beads love and devotion to Our Blessed Mother.

ORDER OF RECITATION

On the first white bead after the medal say the Father of Truth *prayer. On each black bead recite an* Our Father.

On the first three red beads say the Hail Mary *in honor of Saint Charbel's fidelity to the vow of poverty.*

On the second set of red beads say the Hail Mary *in honor of Saint Charbel's fidelity to the vow of chastity.*

281

Chaplet of St. Charbel

On the third set of red beads say the **Hail Mary** *in honor of Saint Charbel's fidelity to the vow of obedience.*

On the three white beads say the **Hail Mary** *in honor of Saint Charbel's love for the Eucharist.*

On the three blue beads say the **Hail Mary** *in honor of Saint Charbel's devotion to our Blessed Mother.*

Conclude with the prayer to obtain graces on the medal.

Father of Truth Prayer

Father of Truth, behold Your Son, a sacrifice pleasing to You. Accept this offering of Him who died for me; behold His blood shed on Golgotha for my salvation. It pleads for me. For His sake, accept my offering. Many are my sins, but greater is Your mercy. When placed on a scale, Your mercy prevails over the weight of the mountains known only to You. Consider the sin and consider the atonement; the atonement is greater and exceeds the sin. Your beloved Son sustained the nails and the lance because of my sins so in His sufferings You are satisfied and I live.

Lord, infinitely holy and glorified in Your saints, You have inspired Charbel, the saint monk, to lead the perfect life of a hermit. We thank You for granting him the blessing and the strength to detach himself from the world so that the heroism of the monastic virtues of poverty, chastity, and obedience might triumph in his hermitage. We beseech You to grant us the grace of loving and serving You, following his example. Almighty God, who have manifested the power of Saint Charbel's intercession through his countless miracles and favors, grant us this grace *(here mention your intention)* which we request from You through his intercession. Amen.

Kateri Indian Rosary

KATERI INDIAN ROSARY

A Chaplet of Prayers dedicated in honor of Blessed Kateri Tekakwitha, the Lily of the Mohawks.

Order of Recitation

1. *Kiss the Cross, and make the Sign of the Cross with it, saying:* In the name of the Father, and of the Son and of the Holy Spirit. Amen. *Ask God to make Kateri a Saint, and petition Kateri to help you in your personal needs.*

2. *Recite an* Our Father *on each of the 8 Brown Beads; a* Hail Mary *on each of the 8 Red Beads; and a* Glory Be *on each of the 8 Crystal Beads.*

3. *Make the Sign of the Cross as above.*

Explanation, Meaning, Intention of the Rosary

The Cross

The Cross is of "Staurolite," Nature's amazing wonder mineral found in the shape of tiny crosses in the mountains of Virginia, North Carolina, and New Mexico.

It is an Indian legend that on the day that Christ died on the Cross, the woodland animals wept, their tiny tears falling upon the earth and crystallizing into these tiny crosses.

The 24 Beads

Blessed Kateri Tekakwitha, "the Lily of the Mohawks," was born in Ossernenon, now known as Auriesville, New York, in 1656. She was born of a Mohawk chief and a Christian mother, but led a life of hardship and pain. Orphaned, disfigured by small pox and plagued by ill health, she remained steadfast to her Christian faith. She practiced acts of kindness and charity to all she met, leading a life of prayer and union with God until her death in 1680 at the age of 24. She was declared blessed by Pope John Paul II in 1980.

The 24 Beads portray Kateri's short, yet fruit-ful 24 years upon this earth.

Brown Beads (8 Our Fathers)

Earth colors were very popular with the Indians. Brown is the predominant color of the earth. It must be one of God's most favorite colors. The moccasins which Kateri and her people wore were brown too.

God the Father gave us this world in perfect order. Ask Blessed Kateri's intercession before God to set this earth, our minds, our bodies, and all our problems in order again.

Red Beads (8 Hail Marys)

Red is the traditional color of love. Love runs in the red blood of all mankind, transcending race and color. God must have had a particular love for this part of the continent when he colored its first inhabitants Red. Indians have an innate love for all mankind as their brothers. Moonstone red is for the high form of love we must have for each other, and the great love that Kateri had for Our Blessed Mother.

Ask Kateri's intercession to Mary to form this kind of love in all our hearts, and to lead us all back to Christ.

Crystal Beads (8 Glory Be's)

Indians believed that the crystal clear lakes and streams were the tears of the Great Spirit.

May the Holy Trinity, the Father, the Son, and the Holy Spirit, through Kateri's prayers, restore the beauty of our waters, skies, forests, and air — the ecology of our entire world.

CHAPLET FOR THE OFFICE OF THE SECULAR FRANCISCAN ORDER

(Traditional Meditation on the Sufferings of Christ)

"We should praise Him and pray to Him day and night, saying 'Our Father, who art in heaven, (Mt 6:9), because we 'must always pray and not lose heart' (Lk 18:1)." (St. Francis: "Letter to All the Faithful")

Begin this chaplet with the Sign of the Cross. *On the solitary bead, pray the* Creed. *While reflecting on each meditation, pray the* Our Father, Hail Mary, *and* Glory Be. *Conclude with St. Francis' Peace Prayer, your own spontaneous prayers, and the* Sign of the Cross.

(To use the meditations as a liturgical office, divide them in half for both morning and evening prayer.)

Meditations:

1. *Jesus shares His last meal with his friends and institutes the Holy Eucharist.*
    Our Father, Hail Mary, Glory Be.

2. *Jesus suffers in agony in the Garden of Gethsemane.*
    Our Father, Hail Mary, Glory Be.

*Chaplet for the Office of the Secular
Franciscan Order*

3. *Jesus is betrayed by Judas.*
   Our Father, Hail Mary, Glory Be.
4. *Jesus is bound and taken to Annas and Caiphas.*
   Our Father, Hail Mary, Glory Be.
5. *Jesus is ridiculed by Herod.*
   Our Father, Hail Mary, Glory Be.
6. *Jesus is forsaken by the people as they choose Barabbas for release.*
   Our Father, Hail Mary, Glory Be.
7. *Jesus is scourged at the pillar and crowned with thorns.*
   Our Father, Hail Mary, Glory Be.
8. *Jesus is condemned to death, death on a Cross.*
   Our Father, Hail Mary, Glory Be.
9. *Jesus carries His Cross and meets his Mother on the road to Calvary.*
   Our Father, Hail Mary, Glory Be.
10. *Jesus is nailed to the Cross and dies.*
    Our Father, Hail Mary, Glory Be.
11. *Jesus is taken down from the Cross and placed in the arms of His Mother.*
    Our Father, Hail Mary, Glory Be.
12. *Jesus is carried and placed in the tomb.*
    Our Father, Hail Mary, Glory Be.

The five knots on the cord represent the five wounds Jesus received at the Crucifixion on His hands, feet and side.

Further guidelines and other meditations for this liturgical office can be found in the Secular Franciscan Companion, *published by Franciscan Herald Press, Chicago.*

Blessed Miguel Pro, S. J.

CHAPLET OF BLESSED MIGUEL PRO, S.J.

"Long live Christ the King!"

These words rang out clearly as a volley of bullets ripped into the body of the brave young priest. It was 1927, and it was a crime to be a Catholic in Mexico. As the long funeral cortege wound its way through the streets of Mexico City, the dead priest's sister began to cry. Her father cautioned, "Dry your tears. Is this how you behave in the presence of a saint?"

Few Americans realize that less than a lifetime ago there was no religious freedom for Catholics in our neighboring country to the south. When the government closed the churches, the bishops called upon the people to make their homes into churches. Miguel Pro, a young Jesuit priest, returned to the land of his birth from safety in exile to minister in secret to the loyal Mexican Catholics. Betrayed through fear, Father Pro was sentenced to death before a firing squad. He forgave his executioners, and said a brief prayer. Refusing the blindfold, he died with the name of Christ on his lips.

Today we call this brave young priest Blessed Miguel Pro.

This chaplet to Blessed Miguel Pro was composed by the well-known Catholic author, Ann Ball, and is included here with her permission.

The chaplet consists of a crucifix followed by six white beads symbolizing Miguel Pro's purity and eleven red beads that recall his martyrdom.

CHAPLET OF BLESSED MIGUEL PRO, S.J.

On the crucifix or medal of Blessed Miguel say:

Blessed Miguel, before your death you told your friend to ask you for favors when you were in heaven. I beg you to intercede for me, and in union with Our Lady and all the angels and saints, to ask Our Lord to grant my petition, provided that it be God's will. *(Here mention your request.)*

Chaplet of Blessed Miguel Pro, S. J.

On the white beads that symbolize his purity:

We honor and adore the triune God. *Glory Be.*

We ask the Holy Spirit for guidance. *Come, Holy Ghost.*

We pray as Jesus taught us to pray. *Our Father.*

We venerate with love the Virgin Mary. *Hail Mary.*

All you angels, bless you the Lord forever. Saint Joseph, Saint *(name of your patron)* and all the saints, pray for us.

On the red beads that symbolize his martyrdom:

Blessed Miguel, high-spirited youth, pray for us. Viva Cristo Rey.

Blessed Miguel, loving son and brother, pray for us. Viva Cristo Rey.

Blessed Miguel, patient novice, pray for us. Viva Cristo Rey.

Blessed Miguel, exile from your homeland, pray for us. Viva Cristo Rey.

Blessed Miguel, prayerful religious, pray for us. Viva Cristo Rey.

Blessed Miguel, sick and suffering, pray for us. Viva Cristo Rey.

Blessed Miguel, defender of workers, pray for us. Viva Cristo Rey.

Blessed Miguel, courageous priest in hiding, pray for us. Viva Cristo Rey.

Blessed Miguel, prisoner in jail, pray for us. Viva Cristo Rey.

Blessed Miguel, forgiver of persecutors, pray for us. Viva Cristo Rey.

Blessed Miguel, holy martyr, pray for us. Viva Cristo Rey.

Imprimatur: Joseph A. Fiorenza
Bishop of Galveston-Houston
August 23, 1995

PADRE PIO NOVENA CHAPLET

This chaplet consists of the prayer for the beatification of Padre Pio combined with the efficacious novena to the Sacred Heart that Padre Pio recited every day.

It is made up of a medal of Padre Pio followed by fifteen beads and ending with a medal of the Sacred Heart.

On the Padre Pio medal say the prayer for the glorification of Padre Pio:

O Jesus, full of grace and charity, victim for sinners, so impelled by love for us that You willed to die on the Cross, I humbly beseech You to glorify in heaven and on earth the Servant of God, Padre Pio of Pietrelcina, who generously participated in Your sufferings, who loved You so much, and labored so faithfully for the glory of Your Heavenly Father and for the good of souls. With confidence I beseech You to grant me, through His intercession, the grace of . . . which I ardently desire.

First Set:

On the first bead say:

O my Jesus, You have said: "Truly I say to you, ask and it will be given you, seek and you will find, knock and it will be opened to you." Behold I knock, I seek and ask for the grace of *(name your request).*

Second bead: Our Father.

Third bead: Hail Mary.

Fourth bead: Glory be to the Father.

Fifth bead: Sacred Heart of Jesus, I place all my trust in You.

Second Set:

First bead: O my Jesus, You have said: "Truly I say to you, if you ask anything of the Father in My Name, He will give it to you." Behold in Your Name I ask the Father for the grace of *(name your request).*

Second bead: Our Father.

Third bead: Hail Mary.

Fourth bead: Glory be to the Father.

Fifth bead: Sacred Heart of Jesus, I place all my trust in You.

Third Set:

First bead: O my Jesus, You have said: "Truly I say to you, heaven and earth will pass away but My words will not pass away." Encouraged by Your infallible words I now ask for the grace of *(name your request).*

Second bead: Our Father.

Third bead: Hail Mary.

Fourth bead: Glory be to the Father.

Fifth bead: Sacred Heart of Jesus, I place all my trust in You.

On the Sacred Heart medal say:

O Sacred Heart of Jesus, for Whom it is impossible not to have compassion on the afflicted, have pity on us miserable sinners and grant us the grace which we ask of You, through the Sorrowful and Immaculate Heart of Mary, Your tender Mother and ours.

Say the Hail Holy Queen *and add:* Saint Joseph, foster father of Jesus, pray for us.

Padre Pio Novena Chaplet

Padre Pio of Pietrelcina

CHAPLETS OF THE SOULS
IN PURGATORY

Obedient even to death (Albrecht Dürer)

THE CHAPLET OR THE ROSARY
FOR THE DEAD

This chaplet for the dead is composed of four decades, that is to say forty beads, in honor and in memory of the forty hours that Our Lord Jesus Christ passed in Limbo, to deliver and conduct to heaven all the souls of the saints who died before Him.

Begin with the De Profundis.

On the large beads say:
Eternal rest give to them, O Lord, and let perpetual light shine upon them. May they rest in peace. Amen. O my God, I believe in Thee because Thou art Truth itself; I hope in Thee because Thou art infinitely merciful; I love Thee with my whole heart and above all things because Thou art infinitely perfect; and I love my neighbor as myself for the love of Thee. I am truly sorry for having sinned because Thou art infinitely good and sin displeases Thee. I firmly resolve, with the help of Thy grace, never more to offend Thee. Amen.

On each of the small beads say:
Sweet Heart of Mary, be my salvation!

Conclude with the De Profundis.

Out of the depths I cry to you, O Lord; O Lord, hear my voice!

Let your ears be attentive to the voice of my supplication.

If you should remember sins, O Lord; O Lord, who could bear it?

But with you is forgiveness, that you may be served with reverence.

I hope in the Lord, my soul hopes in his word;

My soul waits for the Lord, more than watchmen for the dawn.

More than watchmen for the dawn, let Israel wait for the Lord,

For with the Lord is mercy and with him plenteous redemption:

And he shall redeem Israel from all its sins. Eternal rest give to them, O Lord. And let perpetual light shine upon them. May they rest in peace. Amen. O Lord, hear my prayer. And let my cry come to you.

Let us pray. O God, the Creator and Redeemer of all the faithful, grant to the souls of your servants departed the remission of all their sins, that through pious supplications they may obtain the pardon which they have always desired, who lives and reigns, world without end. Amen.

May they rest in peace. Amen.

CHAPLET FOR THE SOULS
IN PURGATORY

1.   O Lord, my Creator and Redeemer, I believe that You, in Your justice, established purgatory for those souls who passed into eternity before having totally satisfied for their debts of guilt or punishment. I also believe that You in Your mercy accept suffrages, particularly the Holy Sacrifice of the Mass, in their behalf to free them. O Lord, enkindle faith in me and infuse in my heart sentiments of pity towards these dear suffering brethren.

Eternal rest, etc.

2.   O Lord Jesus Christ, King of glory, through the intercession of Mary and all the saints, free the souls of the faithful departed from the punishments of purgatory. Do you, St. Michael, standard-bearer of the heavenly army, guide them to the holy light promised by the Lord to Abraham and to his descendants. I offer You, O Lord, sacrifice and prayers of praise. Accept them for these souls and admit them into the joy and light of eternity.

Eternal rest, etc.

3.   O Jesus, my good Master, I beseech You on behalf of the souls towards whom I have serious duties of gratitude, justice, charity

and family ties – parents, spiritual and temporal benefactors, and loved ones. I recommend to You the persons who have greater responsibilities on earth: priests, leaders and lawmakers, superiors, religious. I beseech You also for forgotten souls, and for those who were more devoted to the Holy Eucharist and the Blessed Virgin. O Lord, deign to admit them soon into eternal happiness.

Eternal rest, etc.

4.   O Jesus, Divine Master, I thank You for having come down from heaven to free man from so many evils by Your teachings, holiness and death. I beseech You on behalf of the souls who are in purgatory on account of the press, motion pictures, radio and television. I have confidence that these souls, once freed from their punishments and admitted into eternal joy, will supplicate You on behalf of the modern world, so that the many means You have granted us for elevating this earthly life may also be used as means of apostolate and for life everlasting.

Eternal rest, etc.

5.   O merciful Jesus, by Your sorrowful Passion and by that love which You have for me, I beseech You to cancel the punishments which I deserve in this life or in the next be-

cause of my many sins. Grant me, O Lord, a spirit of penance, purity of conscience, hatred for every deliberate venial sin, and dispositions necessary to gain indulgences. I resolve to help the holy souls in purgatory with suffrages. And You, O infinite Goodness, infuse into my soul a more resolute fervor, so that when my soul is separated from the bonds of my body, it may be admitted into heaven to contemplate You forever.

Our Father, Hail Mary, Eternal rest, etc.

THE ALL SOULS ROSARY

This chaplet is said on an ordinary Rosary.

On the Crucifix say the psalm "Out of the depths":

Out of the depths I cry to you, O Lord; O Lord, hear my voice!

Let your ears be attentive to the voice of my supplication.

If you should remember sins, O Lord; O Lord, who could bear it?

But with you is forgiveness, that you may be served with reverence.

I hope in the Lord, my soul hopes in his word;

My soul waits for the Lord, more than watchmen for the dawn.

More than watchmen for the dawn, let Israel wait for the Lord.

For with the Lord is mercy and with him plenteous redemption.

And he shall redeem Israel from all its sins.

Say the Our Father *on the large beads.*

Say the following Invocation on the small beads:

O good Jesus, have mercy on the souls in purgatory (or the soul or souls of *N.*) and grant to them eternal rest.

Each decade may be offered for a particular intention, by using the following prayers:

First decade: I offer You, my Savior, this first decade for the souls of all my relatives, through the Precious Blood which You shed for them in Your Agony in the Garden of Gethsemane. O good Jesus, have mercy on them!

Our Father. *Repeat the Invocation 10 times.*

Second decade: I offer You, my Savior, this second decade for the souls of all those who have shown me kindness, through the Precious Blood which You shed for them in Your Scourging. O good Jesus, have mercy on them!

Our Father. *Repeat the Invocation 10 times.*

Third decade: I offer You, my Savior, this third decade for the souls of those whom I have at any time offended *(or* for the souls that are the most destitute, *or* for the souls that were the most devoted to the Blessed Virgin Mary), through the Precious Blood which You shed for them in carrying Your Cross to Calvary. O good Jesus, have mercy on them!

Our Father. *Repeat the Invocation 10 times.*

Fourth decade: I offer You, my Savior, this fourth decade for the souls of my friends and companions, through the Precious Blood which You poured forth upon the Cross, and through the sorrows which Mary, our tender Mother, endured at the foot of the Cross. O good Jesus, have mercy on them!

Our Father. *Repeat the Invocation 10 times.*

Fifth decade: I offer You, my Savior, this fifth decade for the soul of my father *(or* mother, *or* N.). I offer You, for this soul so dear to me, the Precious Blood and the sacred water from Your Heart, pierced by the lance. O good Jesus, open to this soul the gate of heaven, and grant me the grace to be reunited with it forever in the bosom of Your goodness.

Our Father. *Repeat the Invocation 10 times:*

O good Jesus, have mercy on the souls in purgatory (or the soul or souls of *N.)* and grant to them eternal rest.

Nihil Obstat: Very Rev. Msgr. Carroll E. Satterfield, S.T.D.
Censor Librorum
Imprimatur: William Donald Borders, D.D.
Archbishop of Baltimore
April 30, 1984

National Shrine of Our Lady of the Miraculous Medal
Perryville, Missouri

The Ruin of Humanity (Albrecht Dürer)

Prayer for a Happy Death

O Holy Father, Saint Benedict, blessed by God both in grace and in name, who whilst rapt in prayer, with thy hands raised to heaven, didst most happily yield thy angelic spirit into the hands of thy Creator, and hast promised zealously to defend against all the snares of the enemy in the last struggle of death those who shall daily remind thee of thy glorious departure and thy heavenly joys; protect me, I beseech thee, O glorious father, this day and every day, by thy holy blessing that I may never be separated from our dear Lord, from the society of thyself and of all the blessed. Through the same Christ our Lord. Amen.

CHAPLETS MAY BE OBTAINED
FROM THE FOLLOWING:

Leaflet Missal Company
976 W. Minnehaha Avenue
St. Paul, Minnesota 55104

The Ravengate Press
P. O. Box 49
Still River, Massachusetts 01467-0049
(800) 344-6736

Christ the King Books and Gifts
5121 Crestway Drive, Suite 111
San Antonio, Texas 78239
(210) 637-5464

Our Lady of Guadalupe Chaplet
Apostolate of Our Lady of Guadalupe
P. O. Box 17634
El Paso, Texas 79917

Little Crown of the Blessed Virgin Mary
Montfort Publications
26 South Saxon Avenue
Bay Shore, New York 11706

Chaplet of Our Lady Star of the Sea
Confraternity of Our Lady Star of the Sea
Central Headquarters
P. O. Box 609
Morgan City, Louisiana 70381

Kateri Indian Rosary
National Blessed Kateri Center
Auriesville, New York 12016

Saint Philomena Chaplet
Universal Living Rosary Association
of Saint Philomena
P. O. Box 1303
Dickinson, Texas 77539

Religious Art, Inc.
276 Greenpoint Ave. 3rd. Fl.
Brooklyn, N.Y. 11222
1-800-991-1211

Precious Blood Chaplet
Monastery of the Precious Blood
700 Bridge Street
Manchester, New Hampshire 03104

Monastery of the Precious Blood
5300 Fort Hamilton Parkway
Brooklyn, New York, 11219

Saint Michael's Chaplet
National Center for Padre Pio, Inc.
Vera Calandra, President
2213 Old Route 100
Barto, Pennsylvania 19504

Cords of Saint Joseph
Elaine Laukaitis
86 Malden Street
Worcester, Massachusetts 01606

HANDMADE ROSARIES & CHAPLETS
Mr. and Mrs. Anthony Conti
11 Dakota Street
Providence, Rhode Island 02904

Mr. William Richer
290 Little Alum Road
Brimfield, Massachusetts 01010

ACKNOWLEDGEMENTS

Chaplet of Divine Mercy
Divine Mercy Center
Stockbridge, Massachusetts

Chaplet of the Precious Blood
Sisters of the Precious Blood
Manchester, New Hampshire

Little Crown of the Blessed Virgin
How to Say Your Rosary with St. Louis De Montfort
Montfort Fathers
Bay Shore, New York

Chaplet of Saint Raphael
Rosary of Praise
Rosary of Our Lady's Tears
The Reparation Society of IHM
Baltimore, Maryland

Saint Jude Chaplet
Panation Trade Co.
Brooklyn, New York

Holy Communion Chaplet
Goldscheider of Vienna
Trenton, New Jersey

The Rosary of the Tears of Blood
Rosa Mystica

Chaplet of Our Lady of Guadalupe
Our Lady of Guadalupe Apostolate
El Paso, Texas

321

Blessed Kateri Indian Rosary
National Blessed Kateri Center
Auriesville, New York

Chaplet of the Holy Angels
JMJ San Damiano Center
Natick, Massachusetts

Beads of St. Anne
Redemptorists

Saint Philomena Chaplet
Universal Living Rosary Association of Saint
Philomena
Dickinson, Texas

Chaplet of Saint Anthony
Rosary of the Seven Joys of the Blessed Virgin
(Franciscan Rosary)
Franciscans

Blessed Sacrament Beads
Blessed Sacrament Fathers

The Brigittine Rosary
Brigittine Fathers

Chaplet of the Five Wounds
Passionists

Rosary of the Seven Sorrows
Servite Fathers

Chaplet of the Holy Spirit (Capuchin)

Rosary of Our Lady of Consolation
Augustinian Fathers

Chaplet of St. Patrick
Holy Rosary Apostolate
Ontario, Canada

The Little Rosary of the Seven Dolors of Mary from the book, *The Mother of God and Her Glorious Feasts*
Tan Books and Publishers
Rockford, Illinois

Beads of the Sacred Heart
from the book, *The Devotion to the Sacred Heart of Jesus*
Tan Books and Publishers
Rockford, Illinois

Chaplet of St. Paul
Daughters of St. Paul
Jamaica Plain, Massachusetts

Chaplet of Our Lady Star of the Sea
Our Lady Star of the Sea Confraternity

Chaplet for Dominican Vocations
Dominicans

Trisagion
Trinitarians

APPENDIX

CHAPLET TO ST. DOMINIC SAVIO

This chaplet was composed by Mrs. Monica Wilcott of Saskatchewan, Canada. She wanted her two young sons to be devoted to a young saint like themselves.

This chaplet is made up of a cross, three white beads and fourteen blue beads.

The three white beads represent the Holy Trinity and also St. Dominic Savio's hard-won purity of heart. The blue beads commemorate the fourteen years of his life and his total devotion to Our Lady.

On the cross say one Glory be *to thank God for the graces Dominic Savio received during his life. On each of the white beads say:* St. Dominic Savio, intercede for me! Ask Our Lady to obtain for me a great increase in:
  First bead: Faith. Hail Mary, *etc.*
  Second bead: Hope. Hail Mary, *etc.*
  Third bead: Charity. Hail Mary, *etc.*

On the center say the first invocation: St. Dominic, you know how hard it is to fight temptation in this life! Consider me as your friend in need. Obtain for me the grace of purity in thought, word, and deed. Help me to improve my self-control!

On each blue bead say St. Dominic's personal motto: Death before sin!

On the center say the second invocation: St. Dominic, you loved Our Lady and went to her with your needs. Go to her and ask the grace to help me remember to ask for her help especially when I am MOST sorely tempted. Obtain for me an increase in love for her, our most tender and loving Mother!

On each blue bead say: Death before sin!

On the center say the third invocation: St. Dominic, you prayed for your family and friends. Please go to Our Lady and intercede for my family and friends, especially *(name them)*, and also for these, my personal intentions.

On each blue bead say: Death before sin!

Concluding prayer: Thank you, St. Dominic, for your intercessions on my behalf. Please pray for me every day of my life. St. Dominic, you struggled in this life with the same temptations to sin as I have, but you never gave up trying. Obtain for me great confidence in Our Lady and the grace of final perseverance, that some day in heaven we may enjoy the delights of her company and sing the praises of the Most Holy Trinity. Through the intercession of Our Lady Mediatrix of all Graces. Amen.